Strindberg
Plays: One

The Father, Miss Julie, The Ghost Sonata

Only recently has Strindberg begun to receive the recognition he deserves. His obsessional treatments of insanity, sexual domination and the psychological warfare between men and women provoked incomprehension and abhorrence during his life-time. But now his plays have taken on a new relevance and directness. He is rightly acclaimed a pioneer of twentieth century theatre and one of the world's great dramatists.

This volume contains three of his most famous plays, spanning twenty years (1887–1907) of prodigious creativity and recurrent personal crises. *The Father* displays Strindberg's suspicion of women at its most implacable. In *Miss Julie* he presents, with startling modernity, the conflict between sexual passion and social position. *The Ghost Sonata*, written in physical pain and spiritual torment, is a phantasmagoric dream play, 'a direct source for the Theatre of the Absurd' (Martin Esslin). A companion volume contains *A Dream Play*, *The Stronger* and *The Dance of Death* and a third volume, containing *Master Olof*, *Creditors* and *To Damascus* (Part I), will be published in May 1991. Meyer is the author of a definitive biography of Strindberg and has written a critically acclaimed play about his life, *Lunatic and Lover*.

Michael Meyer's translations of Strindberg are well known and in 1964 won him the Gold Medal of the Swedish Academy. His translation of *The Father* was seen at the Piccadilly Theatre, London in 1962 and subsequently on both ITV and BBC TV. His translation of *Miss Julie* was performed by the National Theatre, London in 1965 and by the Royal Shakespeare Company in 1971. His translation of *The Ghost Sonata* was screened by BBC-TV in 1962 and again in a new production in 1980. All the translations, as well as his authoritative introductions to each play, have been thoroughly revised and updated by him for this edition.

The painting on the front cover is Edvard Munch's Puberty, *painted in 1895, from the National Gallery in Oslo. The lithograph of Strindberg on the back cover is also by Munch, dated 1896. Both are reproduced by permission of Oslo Kommune Kunstsamlingene, Munch-Museet.*

AUGUST STRINDBERG

Plays: One

The Father
Miss Julie
The Ghost Sonata

Translated from the Swedish
with introductions by
MICHAEL MEYER

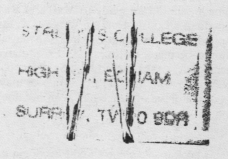
METHUEN DRAMA

Methuen's World Dramatists

English translations and introductions © 1964, 1987
by Michael Meyer
These translations first published in Great Britain in 1964
by Secker & Warburg Limited
First published as a Methuen Paperback in this revised edition
in 1976 by Eyre Methuen Ltd
Reprinted by Methuen London Ltd 1982, 1985, 1987

Reprinted in 1989 by Methuen Drama,
Michelin House, 81 Fulham Road, London SW3 6RB
Reprinted 1990 (twice)

Printed in Great Britain by Cox & Wyman Ltd, Reading

ISBN 0 413 52160 5

Contents

Johan August Strindberg

22 January 1849	Born in Stockholm, the fourth child of a shipping merchant and his former maid-servant.
1853	His father goes bankrupt.
1862	His mother dies. The next year his father marries his housekeeper.
1867	Goes to Upsala University, where he decides to become a doctor.
1869	Fails preliminary examination, leaves University and goes on the stage. Fails at that. Writes his first plays, *A Birthday Gift* and *The Freethinker*.
1870	Returns to Upsala to study modern languages and political science. His fourth play, *In Rome*, is performed briefly at the Royal Theatre in Stockholm.
1872	Leaves Upsala and settles in Stockholm. Tries to go on the stage again, and fails again. Writes first major play, *Master Olof*, but it is not performed for nine years.
1872–4	Journalist in Stockholm.
1874–82	Librarian in Stockholm.
1877	Marries Finnish actress Siri von Essen.
1879	Establishes himself as an author with autobiographical novel, *The Red Room*.
1880–2	Writes historical and pseudo-historical prose works; also *The New State*, a provocative book for which he is venomously attacked.
1883	Leaves Sweden (partly because of these attacks) to spend the next six years abroad in France, Switzerland, Germany and

	Denmark. First theatrical success with *Lucky Peter's Journey* (his ninth play).
1884	Publishes volume of short stories, *Marriage*; is prosecuted for blasphemy; returns to Sweden to face trial; is acquitted.
1886	Writes novel about his childhood, *The Son of a Servant*.
1887	Writes *The Father* in Bavaria. It has a small success in Denmark but fails in Sweden. Also writes rustic novel, *The People of Hemsö*, and, in French, *The Apology of a Fool*, an account of his marriage.
1888	*The Father* staged by Freie Bühne in Berlin; Strindberg becomes known in Germany. He writes *Miss Julie* and *Creditors*, both in Denmark. *Miss Julie* attacked on publication for immorality.
1889	Starts own experimental theatre in Denmark; *Miss Julie* and *Creditors* are staged there, and fail. Theatre goes bankrupt. Strindberg returns to Sweden.
1891	Divorces Siri.
1892	Writes *Playing With Fire* and *The Bond*, his last play for six years. Leaves Sweden for Germany.
1893	Marries Austrian journalist, Frida Uhl. Visits England.
1893-7	Writes many pseudo-scientific articles for alchemistical and other journals, in French.
1894	Leaves Frida and settles in Paris. *Creditors* and *The Father* are staged there, and are well received. Strindberg is lionized but, as always, makes little money.
1894-6	Poor and alone in Paris. Scientific experiments; dabbles in alchemy and tries to make gold. *Inferno* crisis; hovers on brink of insanity.

1896	Emerges from mental crisis and returns to Sweden.
1897	Writes *Inferno* in French, the account of his years of near-madness.
1898	Writes Parts I and II of his dramatic trilogy, *To Damascus*. In the next eleven years he writes thirty-five plays.
1899	Writes *There Are Crimes and Crimes* and *Erik the Fourteenth*, his best historical play.
1900	Meets Norwegian actress, Harriet Bosse, twenty-nine years his junior. Writes *Easter* and *The Dance of Death*, Parts I and II.
1901	Writes *To Damascus*, Part III, and *A Dream Play*. Marries Harriet. She leaves him before the end of the year; returns briefly; then moves away for good (though they remain in contact).
1904–6	He writes no plays. His reputation in decline.
1907	Founds his own Intimate Theatre in Stockholm. Writes four chamber plays for it: *Storm*, *The Burnt House*, *The Ghost Sonata*, *The Pelican*, the first three all within ten weeks. They are coldly received.
1909	Writes last play, *The Great Highway*.
1909–12	Devotes last three years of his life to writing pamphlets on politics, sociology and philosophy.
14 May 1912	Dies in Stockholm of stomach cancer, aged sixty-three.

The Father

A TRAGEDY IN THREE ACTS
1887

Introduction to
The Father

Strindberg wrote *The Father* at Issigatsbühel in Bavaria in January and February of 1887, shortly after his thirty-eighth birthday.

The previous autumn he had completed a play – his first for four years – entitled *The Robbers* (*Marodörer*), which he described to his publisher, Albert Bonnier, as 'a comedy in five acts – the last four written during the past eight days, which doesn't mean they're not good, for I can't write slowly'. This play, which he was later to rewrite under the title of *The Comrades*, was set in Paris and dealt with the marital troubles of a young female painter named Bertha, who smoked cigarettes, wore her hair short and dressed like a man. Bonnier did not much like it, and on 12 January 1887 he wrote to Strindberg that Ludvig Josephson, the director of the New Theatre in Stockholm, had rejected it. 'His refusal does not surprise me', commented Bonnier, 'for, as you know, I have already expressed a similar opinion, *which I still hold*. I fear that these last months you have been living too isolated a life to be able to keep acquainted with public opinion and really understand it, and if you are not willing even to read a country's newspapers I think it must be difficult to go on writing for that country and to partake in its literary polemics.'

Strindberg replied on 6 February: 'One does not *choose* what one writes about. . . . Just now I am preoccupied with this question of women's rights, and shall not drop it until I have investigated and experimented in this field. I have just completed Act One of *The Father*, the first play in the trilogy of which *The Robbers* is the second. I beg you therefore not to reject *The Robbers*, but to make the amendments I have suggested, and in the fulness of time you will see a remarkable work which the wise will still think mad, but which just because of that contains the future. If you reject it, I shall have to go to another publisher, for I won't let myself be silenced in so big and important a matter as this, which has been befogged and made a farce of by such *sometime* men as Ibsen and Bjørnson. In a fortnight, I shall have completed my tragedy, *The Father*. Wait till then.'

The feminist campaign, which Ibsen had championed in such plays as *The Pillars of Society* (1877) and *A Doll's House* (1881) was something to which Strindberg was violently anti-pathetic. His own marriage, with the actress Siri von Essen, was, after ten feverish years, dreadfully on the rocks. He suspected her of being unfaithful to him, both with other men and with a young Danish girl, short-haired and cigarette-smoking like Bertha in *The Robbers*, named Marie David. On 4 January he had explained to Gustaf af Geijerstam: 'I am writing for the theatre now because otherwise the bluestockings will take it over; and the theatre is a weapon', and on 22 January he had complained to Edvard Brandes of Ibsen's 'scandalous attacks on the male sex. I am about to rewrite Act 5 [of *The Robbers*]. Then Part 1 [of the trilogy], *The Father*, and in ten years, when we shall have these women-devils over us with their right to vote and everything, downtrodden men will dig up my trilogy, but will not dare to stage it. . . .[1] I shall fight as long as I have a nerve left in my body, and if they peck me to death you can write a play about "the last man". Actually, my misogyny is entirely theoretical, and I can't live a day without supposing that I warm my soul at the flame of their unconscious, vegetable way of life'.

---

[1] In 1886, just before he wrote *The Father*, Strindberg had been much impressed by an article which he read in a magazine by Paul Lafargue. Lafargue postulated the theory that the family was origi-nally a matriarchy and only became a patriarchy as the result of a long and violent war between the sexes. A return to the matriarchal pattern would involve an equally long and bloody war. At about the time when he was working on *The Father* Strindberg wrote an essay in which he expresses his fear that this battle will mean the defeat of man, and that if this takes place it will herald an age of barbarism. Lafargue refers a great deal in his essay to the *Oresteia* of Aeschylus, and this may have influenced Strindberg into composing *The Father*

He finished *The Father* on 15 February, having apparently completed it in two to three weeks (we do not know the exact date on which he started it). Like so many of Strindberg's plays, it is largely autobiographical, or at any rate an imagined picture of his past and present situation.[1] As long ago as 1872, he had, like the Captain, written to the director of a private asylum asking to be admitted for treatment. 'I have been reading a lot about insanity,' he had told Verner von Heidenstam on 5 October 1886. 'It would seem that all human beings are mad except doctors.' Like the Captain, he had quarrelled with his wife about the future of his two daughters; he wanted them to become nurses, Siri wanted them to train for the stage. (In fact, one became an actress and the other, with dreadful irony when one thinks of Bertha in *The Robbers*, a painter.)

The subject of hypnotism and 'suggestion' was one that deeply interested Strindberg – as, at this same time, it did Ibsen, who had explored it in *Rosmersholm* and was to do so again the next year (1888) in *The Lady from the Sea* and, four years later, in *The Master Builder*. Dr. Gunnar Ollén has noted that Strindberg 'knew of the experiments of Bernheim and the so-called Nancy School in influencing people by suggestion when they are awake, and in the autumn of 1886 he had eagerly devoured Max Nordau's *Paradoxes*, with their demonstrations of the effect of alien suggestion upon ordinarily healthy minds. He knew his Darwin. Man, in his plays, was to be shown as the more refined sex, but also the more debilitated by civilization, and thus doomed to be crushed by the more primitive and stronger female sex. Her weapon of victory was to be not, as in the days of Aeschylus and Shakespeare, poison or dagger, but the much subtler weapon of spiritual murder through suggestion.'

Unlike Ibsen, Strindberg was a revealing correspondent, and

---

more closely according to the classical principles than any of his previous plays.

[1] Almost all the situations in *The Father* reappear in Strindberg's autobiographical novel *The Apology of a Fool*, and some of the lines from the play are repeated word for word.

although he made few references to *The Father* while actually at work on it his letters over the next twelve months contain many passages that throw light upon the state of mind that caused him to write it. On 25 February he remarked to his brother Axel: 'You will know that, as a poet, I blend fiction with reality, and all my misogyny is theoretical, for I couldn't live without the company of women. . . . So you mustn't get depressed when you read *The Father*, for it is a work of fiction. Like *The Robbers*.' A week later he wrote to Georg Lundström: 'I am a misogynist only in theory, and live quite idyllically here in the country alone in a house with six women. My wife and I sing student songs, play backgammon, drink beer and live like newly-weds. We aren't petty, and so never nag each other; I am the most humane of men in everyday matters, and my wife's great virtue is that she isn't small-minded. So we are very happy; and she cooks splendidly and thinks life is wonderful. I keep my play to myself.'

He harps continually on the disservice that Ibsen has done to their sex. 'What would have happened to *A Doll's House*', he asked Edvard Brandes (6 April 1887) 'if Helmer had received a little justice? Or to *Ghosts* if Mr. Alving had been allowed to live and tell the audience that his wife was lying about him? No – just blame everything on them, blacken their names, tread them in the mud so that they haven't a square inch left clean – that makes for good theatre!' And on 3 June he warned the actor August Lindberg, who was negotiating with a Copenhagen theatre to do a season of Ibsen plays: 'You can't go on with Ibsen for long; he probably won't write much more; his *genre* is his speciality and is on the way out. You ought to read what the Germans have to say about *Rosmersholm*!' In this, as in so many other matters, Strindberg proved a bad prophet, for Ibsen was about to embark on his great final sextet of *The Lady from the Sea*, *Hedda Gabler*, *The Master Builder*, *Little Eyolf*, *John Gabriel Borkman* and *When We Dead Awaken*.

That summer Strindberg broke with Siri and applied for a divorce (though they did not finally part until four years later). On 3 September 1887 he wrote a long and hysterical letter to Pehr Staaff: 'Her witchcraft was unbelievable! Notwithstanding her crimes and all her debts she succeeded in making the first man she met believe that I was the guilty one! She got me to imagine for three years that I was ill, got me to imagine I was mad – and everyone pitied and believed her! . . . Remember that Siri tricked me into writing to Forssberg [the family doctor, and an old friend of Strindberg's from their Upsala days] that I believed I was mad. . . . It'll be interesting to see how this drama ends; probably in tragedy. But I won't let her go too soon, or she'll raise an army against me, and female cunning is stronger than male intelligence. Divorce? Yes – then I'll have to sit celibate, masturbating and paying for other men to fornicate with her! That prospect doesn't much amuse me. And her talent for squeezing money out of me is monstrous!'

That autumn Hans Riber Hunderup, the director of the Casino Theatre in Copenhagen, decided to stage *The Father* (which had been rejected by all the Swedish theatres to which it had been offered), and commissioned a young Swedish writer, Axel Lundegård, to translate it and to negotiate with Strindberg for the rights; also, if possible, to persuade him to attend the première. On 17 October Strindberg wrote Lundegård a lengthy and detailed letter in which the precision and clear-sightedness of his observations about the play stand in astonishing contrast to the wildness and woolliness of his remarks on other subjects. After a characteristic opening ('I rejoice to hear from one of the younger generation, who understand what I write and realize that I represent the spirit of our age . . .'), he continued: 'But who is to be the Captain, and what woman is prepared to act Laura? The play can easily be destroyed and become ridiculous! I suggest, though I don't usually interfere in these matters, that the Captain be given to an actor of normally healthy temper who, conscious of his superiority, goes loftily and cynically, almost joyfully, to meet his fate, wrapping himself in death as in a spider's web which he is impotent to tear asunder. A deceived husband is a comic figure in the eyes of the world, and especially to a theatre audience. He must show that he is aware of this, and that he too would laugh if only the man in question were someone other than himself. This is what is *modern* in my tragedy, and alas for me and the clown who acts it if he goes to town and plays an 1887 version of the Pirate King! No screams, no preachings! Subtle, calm, resigned! – the way a normally healthy spirit accepts his fate today, as though it were an erotic passion. Remember that a cavalry officer is always a rich man's son who has had an education,[1] is exacting in his demands upon himself as a social animal, and behaves like a civilized human being even when addressing a common soldier. He mustn't be caricatured into a hidebound military reactionary. He stands above his profession – has seen through it, and turned to science. In particular, he symbolizes for me a masculinity which people have tried to pound or wheedle out of us and transfer to the third sex! It is only when he is with the woman that he is unmanly, because that is how she wants him, and the law of adaptation forces us to play the role that our sexual partner demands. Yes, we sometimes have to act chaste, naïve or ignorant, simply to get our marital rights! . . . As regards appearing personally, I don't believe in that. I've tried it and it hasn't worked. My presence has usually injured my cause, and I am content to stay at my desk. I am gauche, stupid and tactless in company, and too cynical to play the blushing author.'

Despite these and further protestations, however, Strindberg eventually agreed to attend the première, and on 6 November he arrived in Denmark, where he was to spend a harassing and miserable six months. On 12 November, two days before the première, he wrote to Lundegård, to whom he appears to have taken a fancy, warning him that he might 'in a fit of romanticism', absent himself (i.e. commit suicide), and asking the unfortunate young man to act as his executor, listing a series of extraordinary requests. 'Rehabilitate my wife by throwing a cloak of obscurity over everything that has happened, for the children's sake. . . . Force Albert Bonnier to publish Part Four of my autobiography. . . . See that my collected writings are published, when the time is ripe, in Flensburg, Leipzig, Copenhagen or Chicago; *everything* that I have written, every word,

[1] In Bavaria he had met army officers who knew Latin and Greek, and they seem to have corresponded to his idea of a male hero.

from newspapers, almanacs, abroad and at home, including my letters. ... Arrange pensions for my children who, whether they are mine or not, were adopted by me (we don't need to mention my wife). ... Urge Zola to get a publisher for *The Father*, or have it printed in Copenhagen in French ... try to get it acted in Paris. Get in touch with my brother Axel at the Royal Theatre in Stockholm, but don't obey him, for he doesn't understand me and has been talked over by Albert Bonnier and the Younger Generation. ...'

He goes on to the impossibility, if one is a romantic, of living without an ideal. 'Mine was incarnated in a woman, because I was a woman-worshipper. When it fell, I fell! In my letters you will see ... a trusting and credulous fool, who allowed himself to believe anything, even that he was trash, which he wasn't at all – believe anything, so that the crimes of others might be concealed. ... It seems to me as though I walk in my sleep – as though reality and imagination are one. I don't know if *The Father* is a work of the imagination, or if my life has been; but I feel that at a given moment, possibly soon, it will cease, and then I will shrivel up, either in madness and agony, or in suicide. Through much writing my life has become a shadow-play; it is as though I no longer walk the earth, but hover weightless in a space that is filled not with air but with darkness. If light enters this darkness, I shall fall, broken. What is curious is that in a dream which often recurs to me at night I feel that I am flying weightless, and I find this quite natural, as though all conception of right and wrong, true and false, had ceased to exist for me, so that everything that happens, however strange, seems inevitable. Well, I suppose this is the logical consequence of the new philosophy of indeterminism, and perhaps it is because I am unaccustomed to this new intellectual climate that I am amazed and fearful.'

Two days later, on 14 November 1887, the première of *The Father* took place at the Casino Theatre and was, against all expectation, quite a success – partly, no doubt, because the great Georg Brandes had condescended to advise on the production. Hunderup himself played the Captain, with his future wife, Johanne Krum, as Laura. The Danish newspapers

praised the play warmly, and Strindberg found himself referred
to as a genius. The normal fare offered to the Casino's audience
consisted of light comedy and burlesque, and to sugar this
particular pill, which must have perplexed such regular patrons
as had not studied their newspapers, the evening was concluded
with a farce. Even in this promising situation, however,
Strindberg's ill fortune pursued him, for after eleven performances, through no fault of the play, the theatre went bankrupt.
He did not receive a penny from the production, and had to
pawn some of his belongings to see himself and his family
through the worst of the winter.

Largely as a result of the Danish reviews, Ludvig Josephson,
who had previously rejected the play, decided to stage it at his
New Theatre in Stockholm, and on 23 December Strindberg
wrote a long and perceptive letter of advice to the actor who
was to direct and play the lead, August Falck.[1] 'Act the play as
Lindberg acted Ibsen, i.e. not tragedy, not comedy, but somewhere midway between. Don't take it too quickly, as we did
here at the Casino. Rather let it creep forward, quietly, evenly,
until it gathers momentum of its own accord towards the last
act. Exception: the Captain's lines when his obsession has
manifested itself. They should be spoken quickly, abruptly,
repeatedly breaking the atmosphere. Remember: the Captain
is not a coarse soldier, but a scholar who has risen above his
profession. (Think, without copying him, of the late Capt. P.
v. Möller, member of the Academy of History and Literature;
v. Holst the painter, v. Kock the philanthropist, etc.); gentle
in Act 1, a good child; hardens, becomes angry, and at last mad.
Detail: when he enters in Act 3 he is in shirt-sleeves (woollen
shirt), has books under one arm and the saw under the other.
If Laura is played by a young and beautiful woman, she should
be hard, for her appearance will have a softening effect, from
which her influence on her husband gains strength. If she is
played by someone older, she must accentuate the maternal
and somewhat underplay the hardness. The priest is an ordi-

[1] The father of the more famous actor of the same name, who
twenty years later was to be the leading spirit of Strindberg's own Intimate
Theatre in Stockholm.

nary priest, serious, absorbed in the role he finds himself playing, not comic. The doctor is an ordinary doctor, torn between the influence of the woman and his natural sympathy for his fellow man. The daughter must be healthy and captivating, vital, alert, a breath of fresh air in the midst of all this gloom. . . . You will have received a copy showing the cuts. Cut more if you wish! You'll hear at rehearsal what doesn't work. The throwing of the lamp must be devised somehow; here the lamp was of wicker; the glass and shade should be fixed with putty, so that the lamp can be lifted without the glass falling off; it must be thrown past Laura's head out through the door *after* she has retreated through it, so that the audience is left uncertain whether or not it has hit her. Laura screams, and the stage is plunged into darkness. . . . Laura has a good moment in Act 3, Scene 1, when she sits at the secretaire where the Captain had previously sat. If she then repeats or imitates some gesture of the Captain's (e.g., sucking the pen and speaking a line with it between her lips, provided of course that he has done the same), the contrast will prove effective. That's about all I have to say. My greetings to the cast, and every good wish.'

On 12 January 1888 *The Father* received its Swedish première at the New Theatre in Stockholm, and had a mixed reception. 'It can suitably be summed up', wrote one critic, 'in Hamlet's exclamation: "O horrible, O horrible, most horrible!" Any other comment seems superfluous.' The audience began to express its disapproval before the end of the evening, and the play was removed after only nine performances. From this production, Strindberg received approximately £2.

The following year, however, some consolation came with a production at the Freie Bühne in Berlin, the experimental theatre which Otto Brahm had just founded on the model of Antoine's Théâtre Libre in Paris. It was the first time a play by Strindberg had been performed outside Scandinavia, and established him in the country in which his influence and reputation were to remain most constant.

Hunderup, the original producer of *The Father*, having improved his financial position, revived the play on frequent occasions in Denmark, but in the absence of any binding copy-right law Strindberg earned practically nothing from these performances. In 1891, Hunderup took his production to Christiania, where it was seen by at least one notable spectator. Vilhelm Petersen has described in his memoirs how, one hot summer evening, the theatre was almost empty. But in the front row, in lonely majesty, sat Henrik Ibsen, who had been invited to attend and who had just returned to live in Norway after twenty-seven years abroad.[1] After the interval, when there was to have been a farce, Ibsen had gone, and the theatre was left completely empty.

In 1894, Lugné-Poe, Ibsen's champion, staged *The Father* in Paris at his Théâtre de l'Œuvre, the première being attended by Zola, Rodin, Prévost, Sardou, Gauguin and Becque, but (apart from a single performance in 1893), it was to be twenty years before the play was to receive another production in Strindberg's native country, and then only at his own recently-founded Intimate Theatre in Stockholm. There in 1908, it was staged by August Falck, junior, the son of the actor who had been responsible for the ill-fated New Theatre production. This time the play was acclaimed, and ran for seventy-seven performances. Three years later, the Intimate Theatre production was filmed, out of doors in Stockholm 'on an autumn day so cold that the breath of the actors was visible'. Dr. Gunnar Ollén, who saw the film, comments that the style of acting is, for the period, surprisingly restrained, partly, per-haps, because the company was used to playing in so tiny an auditorium.

The same year, 1911, *The Father* was performed in London, first in Yiddish at the Pavilion Theatre in Whitechapel and

---

[1] More accurately, he had returned to Norway for a holiday, but in fact stayed for the remaining fifteen years of his life. Unfortunately his opinion of *The Father* is not on record. Later he kept a painting of Strindberg on his study wall, not, he explained, because of any sympathy or friendship with either the painter or Strindberg, but because 'I am now not able to write a word without having that madman staring down at me!'

subsequently in English at the little Rehearsal Theatre in Maiden Lane. *The Times* remarked that Strindberg seemed 'extraordinarily naïve in some of his dramatic processes', and *The Academy* asked: 'Why use the theatre for unrelieved depression and brutal aspects of human nature and relationships exploited in the name of art?' It might with luck have been seen twenty years earlier in London; J. T. Grein, the founder of the Independent Theatre which introduced Ibsen to English audiences, subsequently put on record (*The Sketch*, 31 July 1929) that he 'tried in vain to cast it for our Independent Theatre, because all the women I approached to play the Captain's wife rebuffed me with the same answer: "You do not expect me to play that awful part?"'

In 1912 *The Father* was produced in New York, with Warner Oland in the title role, but the only two countries in which the play really succeeded before the First World War were Germany and Russia. By 1914 it had been produced in Berlin, Hamburg, Leipzig, Munich, Nuremberg, Stuttgart, Graz and Brunn, as well as twice in Vienna. In 1904 it was staged in St. Petersburg, and in 1905 in Moscow; the latter production was so successful that it toured many of the Russian cities, and in Nijni Novgorod the police had to remove four women who had been overcome with hysterics during the last act.

After the First World War, the climate of theatrical taste had changed, and *The Father* came into its own in many countries. In London, in 1927, Robert Loraine achieved a great success at the Everyman Theatre, which he repeated when the play was transferred to the Savoy[1]. In 1929 Malcolm Morley played it in modern dress, again at the Everyman; and three weeks later, by what seems to have been a generous arrangement, Morley produced the play at the Apollo Theatre in period costume, with Loraine back in his old part. Since the Second World War, *The Father* has twice been finely acted in London,

[1] When Loraine first read the play to his wife, she fell on her knees half-way through to assure him that his children were his own and that he was not to believe a word of the play. Loraine commented: 'If it upsets you like that, there must be something in it.'

in 1953 by Wilfrid Lawson and in 1964 by Trevor Howard. Lawson, in particular, gave an unforgettable performance. It has been seen four times on British television, in 1957 (Basil Sydney, Phyllis Calvert and Mary Merrall; directed by Peter Cotes), 1962 (Robert Shaw, Daphne Slater and Wynne Clark; directed by Alan Bridges), 1968 (Patrick Wymark, Dorothy Tutin and Sybil Thorndike; directed by Dennis Vance) and 1985 (Colin Blakely, Dorothy Tutin, Irene Handl and Edward Fox; directed by Kenneth Ives).

The Father

This translation of *The Father* was first performed on 14 January 1964 at the Piccadilly Theatre, London. The cast was:

THE CAPTAIN	Trevor Howard
LAURA, his wife	Joyce Redman
BERTHA, their daughter	Jo Maxwell Muller
DR. ÖSTERMARK	Nigel Stock
THE PASTOR	Alfred Burke
THE NURSE	Gwen Nelson
NÖJD, a servant	Trevor Peacock
BATMAN	Malcolm Tierney

Directed by Casper Wrede

On 4 March 1968 it was performed on Associated Television. The cast was:

THE CAPTAIN	Patrick Wymark
LAURA	Dorothy Tutin
BERTHA	Nicola Jenkins
DR. ÖSTERMARK	David William
THE PASTOR	Brian Wilde
THE NURSE	Sybil Thorndike
NÖJD	John Malcolm
BATMAN	Gil Sutherland

Directed by Dennis Vance

ACT ONE

A room in the CAPTAIN'S *house. Upstage right, a door. In the centre of the room is a large round table, with newspapers and magazines. On the right, a leather sofa and a table. In the right-hand corner, a concealed door. On the left, a secretaire, with an ornamental clock on it, and a door which leads to the rest of the house. There are weapons on the wall; rifles and game-bags. By the door, clothes-hangers with military tunics on them. On the large table a lamp is burning.*

Scene 1

The CAPTAIN *and the* PASTOR *on the leather sofa. The* CAPTAIN *is in undress uniform, with riding-boots and spurs. The* PASTOR *is in black, with a white stock, but without his clerical bands. He is smoking a pipe.*

The CAPTAIN *rings. The* BATMAN *enters.*

BATMAN. Sir?
CAPTAIN. Is Nöjd out there?
BATMAN. He's waiting for orders in the kitchen, sir.
CAPTAIN. In the kitchen again! Send him here at once!
BATMAN. Sir! (*Goes.*)
PASTOR. What's the matter now?
CAPTAIN. Oh, he's been mucking about with the kitchen-maid again. Damned nuisance, he is!
PASTOR. Nöjd? Why, you had trouble with him last year too!
CAPTAIN. You remember? Perhaps you'd give him a friendly talking-to – that might have some effect. I've sworn at him, and given him a tanning, but it doesn't do any good.
PASTOR. So you want me to read him a sermon! Do you think

27

the word of God will have any effect on a cavalryman?
CAPTAIN. Well, it doesn't have any effect on me, as you know –
PASTOR. Yes, I know!
CAPTAIN. But on him – ? Try, anyway.

Scene 2

The CAPTAIN. *The* PASTOR. NÖJD.

CAPTAIN. Well, Nöjd, what have you been up to now?
NÖJD. God bless you, Captain, I couldn't tell you before his Reverence.
PASTOR. Come, come, don't be bashful, my lad!
CAPTAIN. Own up, or you know what'll happen!
NÖJD. Well, sir, it was like this, you see. We was dancing up at Gabriel's, and then, yes, well, Lars said –
CAPTAIN. What's Lars got to do with it? Stick to the facts!
NÖJD. Well, Emma suggested we should go to the barn.
CAPTAIN. I see! So it was Emma who seduced you!
NÖJD. Well, it wasn't far off. And I'll say this – if a girl ain't willing, she don't run no danger.
CAPTAIN. Out with it! Are you the child's father or not?.
NÖJD. How can I tell?
CAPTAIN. What! You can't tell!
NÖJD. Well, you can never be sure.
CAPTAIN. Weren't you the only one, then?
NÖJD. I was that time, but that don't mean to say I was the only one.
CAPTAIN. Are you saying Lars is to blame? Is that it?
NÖJD. It ain't easy to say who's to blame.
CAPTAIN. But you've told Emma you want to marry her.
NÖJD. Yes, well, you have to tell them that.
CAPTAIN (*to* PASTOR). This is monstrous!
PASTOR. It's the old story. Now, look here, Nöjd, surely you're man enough to know whether you're the father!
NÖJD. Well, I did go with her, but, as your Reverence well knows, that don't necessarily mean anything need happen.

PASTOR. Look here, my lad, don't start trying to evade the issue! You surely don't want to leave the girl alone with the child! Of course we can't force you to marry her, but you must accept responsibility for the child. That you shall!

NÖJD. All right, but Lars must pay his share.

CAPTAIN. Oh, very well, it'll have to go to court. I can't unravel the rights and wrongs of this, and I don't feel inclined to try. Right, get out!

PASTOR. Nöjd! One moment. Hm! Don't you regard it as dishonourable to leave a girl high and dry like that with a child? Eh? Well? Don't you feel such behaviour would be – hm – ?

NÖJD. Oh, yes, if I knew I was the child's father. But that's something a man can never be sure of, your Reverence. And it's no joke spending your whole life sweating for someone else's children. I'm sure you and the Captain'll both appreciate that.

CAPTAIN. Get out!

NÖJD. Sir! (*Goes.*)

CAPTAIN. And keep out of the kitchen, you rascal, damn you!

Scene 3

CAPTAIN. Well, why didn't you lay into him?

PASTOR. What? I thought I spoke very strictly.

CAPTAIN. Oh, you just sat there mumbling to yourself.

PASTOR. To be honest, I don't know what one ought to say. It's bad luck on the girl, yes. But it's bad luck on the boy, too. Suppose he isn't the father? The girl can suckle the child for four months at the orphanage, and then she'll be shot of him, but the boy can't dodge his responsibility like that. She'll get a good job afterwards in some decent home, but if he gets thrown out of his regiment, he's finished.

CAPTAIN. Yes, I wouldn't like to be the magistrate who has to judge this case. I don't suppose the lad's completely innocent – one can't be sure. But one thing you can be sure of. The girl's guilty – if you can say anyone's guilty.

PASTOR. Yes, yes! I'm not condemning anyone! But what were we speaking about when this blessed business intervened? Bertha's confirmation, wasn't it?

CAPTAIN. It's not just her confirmation. It's the whole question of her upbringing. This house is stuffed with women every one of whom wants to bring up my child. My mother-in-law wants to make her a spiritualist, Laura wants her to be a painter, her governess wants her to be a Methodist, old Margaret wants her to be a Baptist, and the maids are trying to get her into the Salvation Army. Well, you can't patch a soul together like a damned quilt. I have the chief right to decide her future, and I'm obstructed whichever way I turn. I've got to get her out of this house.

PASTOR. You've too many women running your home.

CAPTAIN. You needn't tell me that. It's like a cage full of tigers – if I didn't keep a red-hot iron in front of their noses, they'd claw me to the ground the first chance they got. Yes, you can laugh, you old fox! It wasn't enough that I married your sister, you had to palm your old stepmother off on me too!

PASTOR. Well, good heavens, one can't have one's stepmother living under one's roof.

CAPTAIN. But one's mother-in-law is all right? Yes, under someone else's roof!

PASTOR. Well, well. We all have our cross to bear.

CAPTAIN. Yes, but I've a damned sight too many. I've got my old nurse too, and she treats me as though I was still in a bib! Oh, she's a dear old soul, heaven knows, but she doesn't belong here!

PASTOR. You should keep your women in their place, Adolf. You let them rule you.

CAPTAIN. My dear brother-in-law, will you kindly tell me how one keeps women in their place?

PASTOR. To speak frankly, Laura – I know she's my sister, but – well, she was always a little difficult.

CAPTAIN. Oh, Laura has her moods, but she's not too bad.

PASTOR. Ah, come on! I know her!

CAPTAIN. Well, she's had a romantic upbringing, and has a

little difficulty in accepting life, but, after all, she is my wife –

PASTOR. And is therefore the best of women. No, Adolf, she's the biggest stone round your neck.

CAPTAIN. Yes, well, anyway, now the whole house has become impossible. Laura doesn't want to let Bertha out of her sight. But I can't let her stay in this asylum.

PASTOR. So? Laura won't – ? Hm, then I'm afraid things aren't going to be easy. When she was a child, she used to lie absolutely still like a corpse until she'd got what she wanted. And when she'd got it, she'd give it back, explaining that it wasn't the *thing* she wanted, simply the fact of having her will.

CAPTAIN. I see, she was like that already, was she? Hm! She gets so emotional sometimes that I become frightened, and wonder if she isn't – well – sick.

PASTOR. But what is it you want for Bertha that she finds so unacceptable? Can't you meet each other halfway?

CAPTAIN. You mustn't imagine I want to build the child into a prodigy, or a copy of myself. But I don't want to play the pimp and educate her just simply for marriage – if I do that and she stays single, she'll become one of these embittered spinsters. On the other hand, I don't want to train her for some masculine vocation that'll need years of study and be completely wasted if she does get married.

PASTOR: What do you want, then?

CAPTAIN. I'd like her to become a teacher. Then, if she stays single she'll be able to look after herself, and won't be worse off than these wretched schoolmasters who have to support a family. And if she does marry, she can use the knowledge she's gained in bringing up her own children. That's logical, isn't it?

PASTOR. Perfectly. But hasn't she shown a great talent for painting? Wouldn't it be bad for her to repress that?

CAPTAIN. No, no. I've shown her efforts to a prominent artist, and he says it's only the kind of thing people learn to do at schools. But then some young ass came here last summer who knew more about such matters, and said she was a genius – and as far as Laura was concerned, that settled it.

PASTOR. Was he in love with the girl?

CAPTAIN. I presume so.

PASTOR. Then God help you, my dear fellow, for there'll be nothing you can do about that! But this is a sad business, and of course Laura has allies – in there.

CAPTAIN. Oh, yes, never you fear! The whole household is up in arms – and, between you and me, they're not fighting strictly according to the rules of chivalry.

PASTOR (*gets up*). Do you think I haven't been through all this?

CAPTAIN. You too?

PASTOR. Are you surprised?

CAPTAIN. But the worst is, it seems to me Bertha's future is being decided in there from motives of hatred. They keep dropping hints that men will see that women can do this and do that. Man versus woman, that's their theme, all day long. Must you go now? No, stay for supper. I can't offer you much, but, did I tell you, I'm expecting the new doctor to pay a call? Have you seen him?

PASTOR. I caught a glimpse of him on my way here. He looks a pleasant, straightforward chap.

CAPTAIN. Does he? Good! Think he might be on my side?

PASTOR. Who knows? It depends how much he's had to do with women.

CAPTAIN. Oh, come on, do stay!

PASTOR. No thanks, my dear fellow. I've promised to be home for supper, and my good lady gets so worried if I'm late.

CAPTAIN. Worried? Angry, you mean! Well, as you wish. Let me give you a hand with your coat.

PASTOR. It's certainly very cold tonight. Thank you. You want to look after yourself, Adolf. You look nervy.

CAPTAIN. Do I?

PASTOR. You're not quite yourself, are you?

CAPTAIN. Has Laura given you that idea? She's been treating me like a budding corpse for twenty years.

PASTOR. Laura? No, no, I just wondered – Take care of yourself! That's my advice. Well, goodbye, old chap. But didn't you want to talk to me about the confirmation?

CAPTAIN. No, that'll have to take its course. Chalk that one up to society's conscience. I don't intend to be a martyr for the sake of truth. I'm past all that. Goodbye! Give my regards to your wife!

PASTOR. Goodbye, brother! Give mine to Laura!

Scene 4

The CAPTAIN. *Then* LAURA.

CAPTAIN (*opens the secretaire, sits down at it and starts counting*). Thirty-four – nine – forty-three – seven eights – fifty-six.

LAURA (*enters from the main part of the house*). Would you mind –

CAPTAIN. In a moment. Sixty-six, seventy-one, eighty-four, eighty-nine, ninety-two, one hundred. What is it?

LAURA. Perhaps I'm disturbing you.

CAPTAIN. Not at all. The housekeeping money, I suppose?

LAURA. Yes. The housekeeping money.

CAPTAIN. Leave the bills there, and I'll go through them.

LAURA. Bills?

CAPTAIN. Yes.

LAURA. Oh, you want bills now?

CAPTAIN. Of course I want bills. We are financially embarrassed, and if things come to a head I've got to be able to produce accounts. Otherwise I can be punished as a negligent debtor.

LAURA. It isn't my fault if we're financially embarrassed.

CAPTAIN. That's just what the bills will establish.

LAURA. I'm not to blame if our tenant won't pay the lease of his farm.

CAPTAIN. Who recommended him? You. Why did you recommend such a – what shall we call him? Drone?

LAURA. If he's such a drone, why did you take him?

CAPTAIN. Because you wouldn't let me eat in peace, sleep in peace or work in peace until you'd got him here. You wanted

33

to have him because your brother wanted to be rid of him, your mother wanted to have him because I didn't want to have him, the governess wanted to have him because he was a Methodist, and old Margaret wanted to have him because she'd known his grandmother since they were children. That is why we took him, and if I hadn't I should now be either sitting in an asylum or lying in the family vault. However, here is your household allowance, and some pin money. You can give me the bills later.

LAURA (*curtseys*). Thank you, sir. Do you keep bills for your private expenses?

CAPTAIN. That's none of your business.

LAURA. True; no more than my child's upbringing. Have you gentlemen reached a decision now, after your evening session?

CAPTAIN. I had already made my decision. I merely wished to impart it to the only friend whom I and my family have in common. Bertha is to live in town. She will leave in a fortnight.

LAURA. And with whom is she to live, if I may be allowed to ask?

CAPTAIN. I have arranged for her to lodge with my lawyer, Mr. Saevberg.

LAURA. That freethinker!

CAPTAIN. The law states that a child is to be brought up in her father's faith.

LAURA. And the mother has no say in the matter?

CAPTAIN. None. She has sold her birthright by legal contract, and has surrendered all her claims. In return, the husband supports her and her children.

LAURA. So she has no rights over her own child?

CAPTAIN. None whatever. Once you have sold something, you can't get it back and keep the money.

LAURA. But if the father and mother should agree on a compromise – ?

CAPTAIN. How is that possible? I want her to live in town, you want her to stay at home. The arithmetical mean would be that she should live on the railway line, halfway between. This is a situation which cannot be resolved by compromise.

LAURA: Then it must be resolved by force. What did Nöjd want here?

CAPTAIN. That is a military secret.

LAURA. The whole kitchen knows.

CAPTAIN. Then you should.

LAURA. I do.

CAPTAIN. And have passed judgement?

LAURA. The law is quite explicit on the matter.

CAPTAIN. The law is not explicit as to who is the child's father.

LAURA. No. But one usually knows.

CAPTAIN. Wise men say one can never be sure about such things.

LAURA. Not be sure who is a child's father?

CAPTAIN. They say not.

LAURA. How extraordinary! Then how can the father have all these rights over her child?

CAPTAIN. He only has them if he accepts responsibility for the child – or has the responsibility forced upon him. And in marriage, of course, the question of paternity does not arise.

LAURA. Never?

CAPTAIN. I should hope not.

LAURA. But if the wife has been unfaithful?

CAPTAIN. That is not relevant to our discussion. Are there any other questions you want to ask me?

LAURA. None whatever.

CAPTAIN. Then I shall go to my room. Please be so good as to inform me when the Doctor comes. (*Shuts the secretaire and rises.*)

LAURA. Very well.

CAPTAIN (*going through concealed door right*). The moment he arrives! I don't wish to seem discourteous. You understand? (*Goes.*)

LAURA. I understand.

Scene 5

LAURA *alone. She looks at the banknotes she is holding in her hand.*

GRANDMOTHER (*offstage*). Laura!
LAURA. Yes?
GRANDMOTHER. Is my tea ready?
LAURA (*in the doorway left*). I'll bring it in a moment.

Goes towards the door upstage. Just before she reaches it, the BATMAN *opens it.*

BATMAN. Dr. Östermark!
DOCTOR (*enters*). Mrs. Lassen?
LAURA (*goes to greet him, and stretches out her hand*). How do you do, Doctor! Welcome to our home. The Captain is out, but he will be back shortly.
DOCTOR. Please forgive me for coming so late. I've already had to visit some patients.
LAURA. Won't you sit down?
DOCTOR. Thank you, Mrs. Lassen, thank you.
LAURA. Yes, there's a lot of illness around here just now. However, I do hope you'll be happy here. We lead such a lonely life out here in the country, so it's important for us to have a doctor who takes an interest in his patients. And I've heard many flattering reports of you, so I hope we shall see a good deal of each other.
DOCTOR. You are too kind, Mrs. Lassen. But I trust, for your sake, that my visits will not always have to be professional! Your family enjoys good health – ?
LAURA. We've never had any serious illnesses, I am glad to say. But things aren't quite as they should be –
DOCTOR. Indeed?
LAURA. I'm afraid they are not at all as we could wish.
DOCTOR. Really? You alarm me!
LAURA. There are certain domestic matters which a woman's

honour and conscience require her to conceal from the world –

DOCTOR. But not from her doctor.

LAURA. Precisely. So I feel it is my painful duty to be quite open with you from the start.

DOCTOR. Could we not postpone this conversation until I have had the pleasure of making the Captain's acquaintance?

LAURA. No. You must hear what I have to say before you see him.

DOCTOR. It concerns him, then?

LAURA. Yes – my poor, beloved husband!

DOCTOR. You alarm me, Mrs. Lassen. Believe me, I am deeply touched by your distress.

LAURA (*takes out her handkerchief*): My husband is mentally unbalanced. Now you know. You will be able to judge for yourself later.

DOCTOR. What! But I have read with admiration the Captain's excellent dissertations on mineralogy, and have always received the impression of a powerful and lucid intelligence.

LAURA. Indeed? I should be most happy if it could be proved that we have all been mistaken.

DOCTOR. It is of course possible that his judgement may be disturbed where other matters are concerned. Pray proceed.

LAURA. That is what we fear. You see, sometimes he has the most extraordinary ideas, which we would gladly indulge if they didn't threaten the existence of his whole family. For example, he has a mania for buying things.

DOCTOR. That is rather unfortunate. But what does he buy?

LAURA. Whole crates of books, which he never reads.

DOCTOR. Well, it isn't so unusual for a scholar to buy books.

LAURA. You don't believe me?

DOCTOR. Yes, Mrs. Lassen, I am sure that what you say is true.

LAURA. But is it reasonable for a man to claim that he can see in a microscope what is happening on another planet?

DOCTOR. Does he say that?

LAURA. Yes.

DOCTOR. In a microscope?

LAURA. Yes, in a microscope.

DOCTOR. If that is so, it is indeed unfortunate –

LAURA. *If* it is so! You don't believe me, Doctor. And I sit here telling you all our family secrets –

DOCTOR. Now please listen, Mrs. Lassen. I am honoured that you should confide in me. But you understand that as a doctor, I must investigate the matter thoroughly before I can make a diagnosis. Has the Captain shown any symptoms of capriciousness or vacillation?

LAURA. Any symptoms! We've been married for twenty years, and he has never yet taken a decision without reversing it.

DOCTOR. Is he stubborn?

LAURA. He always insists on having his own way, but once he has got it he loses interest and begs me to decide.

DOCTOR. This is unfortunate. I must observe him closely. You see, my dear Mrs. Lassen, will is the backbone of the mind. If the will is impaired, the mind crumbles.

LAURA. God knows I've done my best to meet his wishes during all these long years of trial. Oh, if you knew the things I have had to put up with! If you knew!

DOCTOR. Mrs. Lassen, your distress moves me deeply, and I promise you I will see what can be done. But after what you have told me, I must ask you one thing. Avoid touching on any subject that might excite your husband. In a sick brain, fancies grow like weeds, and can easily develop into obsessions or even monomania. You understand?

LAURA. You mean I must take care not to awake his suspicions?

DOCTOR. Exactly. A sick man is receptive to the slightest impression, and can therefore be made to imagine anything.

LAURA. Really? Yes, I understand. Yes. Yes. (*A bell rings within the house.*) Excuse me, my mother wishes to speak with me. Wait a moment – this must be Adolf!

Scene 6

The DOCTOR. *The* CAPTAIN *enters through the concealed door.*

CAPTAIN. You here already, Doctor? Delighted to meet you!

DOCTOR. Good evening, Captain. It is a great honour for me to make the acquaintance of so distinguished a scientist.

CAPTAIN. Oh, nonsense. My military duties don't allow me much time for research. All the same, I think I'm on to a new discovery.

DOCTOR. Indeed?

CAPTAIN. Yes, I've been submitting meteorites to spectral analysis, and I've discovered carbon! Evidence of organic life! What do you say to that?

DOCTOR. You can see that in the microscope?

CAPTAIN. Microscope? Good God, no – spectroscope!

DOCTOR. Spectroscope? Yes, of course, I mean spectroscope. Well, then, you'll soon be able to tell us what is happening on Jupiter.

CAPTAIN. Not what *is* happening, but what *has* happened. If only that damned shop in Paris would send those books! I really believe all the booksellers in the world have entered into a conspiracy against me. Would you believe it, for two months I haven't had a reply to a single order, letter or even telegram! I just don't understand it. It's driving me mad.

DOCTOR. Oh, that's just common laziness. You mustn't take it too seriously.

CAPTAIN. Yes, but, damn it, I won't be able to get my thesis ready in time – I know there's a fellow in Berlin working on the same lines. Still, we haven't met to talk about that, but about you. If you'd care to live here, we have a small apartment in the wing – or would you rather take over your predecessor's lodgings?

DOCTOR. Just as you please.

CAPTAIN. No, as *you* please. Say, now.

DOCTOR. You must decide, Captain.

CAPTAIN. No, no, I can't decide. You must say what you want. I've no feelings in the matter, no feelings at all.

DOCTOR. Yes, but I can't decide –

CAPTAIN. For God's sake, man, say what you want! I've no inclinations in the matter, I couldn't care less what you do! Are you such a nitwit that you don't know what you want? Answer, or I'll get angry!

DOCTOR. If I must decide, then I'll live here!

CAPTAIN. Good! Thank you. Oh – ! Forgive me, Doctor, but nothing annoys me so much as to hear people say it's all the same to them!

He rings. The NURSE *enters.*

CAPTAIN. Oh, is it you, Margaret? Tell me, old dear, do you know if the wing is ready for the doctor?

NURSE. Yes, sir, it's all ready.

CAPTAIN. Good. Then I won't keep you, Doctor – I expect you're tired. Good night. I'll look forward to seeing you again tomorrow.

DOCTOR. Good night, Captain.

CAPTAIN. I suppose my wife told you a few things about conditions here, to put you in the picture?

DOCTOR. She did mention one or two details she thought it might be useful for a stranger to know. Good night, Captain.

Scene 7

The CAPTAIN. *The* NURSE.

CAPTAIN. What do you want, old darling? Is something the matter?

NURSE. Now, listen, Mr. Adolf, pet.

CAPTAIN. What is it, Margaret? Speak out, my dear. You're the only one I can listen to without getting spasms.

NURSE. Now, listen, Mr. Adolf. Why don't you go halfway to meet madam about the child? Remember, she's a mother.

CAPTAIN. Remember I'm a father, Margaret.

NURSE. Now, now, now! A father has other things beside his child, but a mother has nothing. She's only got her child.

CAPTAIN. Exactly. She has only one burden, but I have three, including hers. Do you think I'd have stayed a soldier all my life if I hadn't been saddled with her and her child?

NURSE. Oh, I didn't mean that.

CAPTAIN. No, I'm sure you didn't. You're trying to put me in the wrong.

NURSE. Surely you think I want what's best for you, Mr. Adolf?

CAPTAIN. Yes, yes, my dear, I'm sure you do. But you don't know what's best for me. You see, it isn't enough for me to have given the child life. I want to give it my soul too.

NURSE. Well, I don't understand that. But I still think you ought to be able to come to some agreement.

CAPTAIN. You are not my friend, Margaret.

NURSE. I? Why, Mr. Adolf, how can you say such a thing? Do you think I can forget you were my baby when you were little?

CAPTAIN. Have *I* ever forgotten it, my dear? You've been like a mother to me – you've supported me, up to now, when everyone's been against me – but now, when I need you most, now you betray me and go over to the enemy.

NURSE. Enemy!

CAPTAIN. Yes, enemy! You know how things are in this house. You've seen it all, from the beginning.

NURSE. Yes, I've seen enough. Blessed Jesus, why must two human beings torment the life out of each other? You're both so good and kind – madam's never like that to me or anyone else.

CAPTAIN. Only to me. Yes, I know. But I'm telling you, Margaret – if you desert me now, you are committing a sin. A web is being spun around me here, and that doctor is not my friend.

NURSE. Oh, Mr. Adolf, you think bad of everyone. But that's because you don't follow the true faith. That's the cause of it.

CAPTAIN. And you've found the only true faith, you and your Baptists. Aren't you lucky!

NURSE. Well, I'm luckier than you, Mr. Adolf. And happier. Humble your heart, and you'll see. God will make you happy and you'll love your neighbour.

CAPTAIN. It's extraordinary – as soon as you start talking about God and love, your voice becomes hard and your eyes fill with hatred. No, Margaret, you haven't found the true faith.

NURSE. Ah, you're proud. All your learning won't get you far at the Day of Judgement.

CAPTAIN. How arrogantly thou speakest, O humble heart! Yes, I know learning means nothing to animals like you.

NURSE. Shame on you! Never mind. Old Margaret loves her big, big boy best of all, and when the storm comes he'll creep back to her like the good little child he is.

CAPTAIN. Margaret! Forgive me, but – believe me, there's no one here who loves me except you. Help me. I feel something is going to happen here – I don't know what, but there's something evil threatening – (*There is a scream from within the house.*) What's that? Who's screaming?

Scene 8

The CAPTAIN. *The* NURSE. BERTHA *enters.*

BERTHA. Father, father! Help me! Save me!

CAPTAIN. What is it, my beloved child? Tell me.

BERTHA. Help me! I think she wants to hurt me!

CAPTAIN. Who wants to hurt you? Tell me. Tell me.

BERTHA. Grandmamma. But it was my fault. I played a trick on her.

CAPTAIN. Tell me about it.

BERTHA. But you mustn't say anything! Promise you won't!

CAPTAIN. Very well. But tell me what it is.

The NURSE *goes.*

BERTHA. Well – in the evenings, she turns down the lamp and sits me down at the table with a pen and paper. And then she says that the spirits are going to write.

CAPTAIN. What! Why haven't you told me about this before?

BERTHA. Forgive me – I didn't dare. Grandmamma says the spirits take their revenge if anyone talks about them. And then the pen writes, but I don't know if it's me. And sometimes it goes all right, but sometimes it won't move at all. And when I'm tired, nothing comes – but it's *got* to come! And tonight I thought I was writing well, but then grandmamma said I was copying from some old poem and playing a trick on her – and then she became so horribly angry!

CAPTAIN. Do you believe that spirits exist?

BERTHA. I don't know.

CAPTAIN. But I know they do not!

BERTHA. But grandmamma says you don't understand, and that you have much worse things, that can see what's happening on other planets.

CAPTAIN. She says that, does she? What else does she say?

BERTHA. She says you can't work magic.

CAPTAIN. I haven't said I can. You know what meteorites are? Yes, stones that fall from other heavenly bodies. I can study them and say whether they contain the same elements as our earth. That's all I can see.

BERTHA. But grandmamma says there are things that she can see but you can't.

CAPTAIN. Well, she's lying.

BERTHA. Grandmamma doesn't tell lies.

CAPTAIN. How do you know?

BERTHA. Then mother would be lying too.

CAPTAIN. Hm!

BERTHA. If you say mother's lying, I'll never believe you again!

CAPTAIN. I haven't said that, and you must believe me when I tell you that your happiness and your whole future depend on your leaving this house. Would you like that? Would you like to go and live in town, and learn something useful?

BERTHA. Oh, I'd so love to live in town and get away from here – anywhere! As long as I can see you sometimes – often! In there everything's so gloomy, so horrible, like a winter night – but when you come, father, it's like throwing open the window on a spring morning!

CAPTAIN. My child! My child!

BERTHA. But, father, you must be nice to mother, do you hear? She cries so often.

CAPTAIN. Hm! So you want to go and live in town?

BERTHA. Yes! Yes!

CAPTAIN. But if your mother doesn't want you to?

BERTHA. But she must!

CAPTAIN. But if she doesn't?

BERTHA. Well, then – I don't know. But she must! She must!

CAPTAIN. Will you ask her?

BERTHA. You must ask her, nicely. She doesn't pay any attention to me.

CAPTAIN. Hm! Well, if you want it and I want it, and she doesn't want it, what shall we do then?

BERTHA. Oh, then everything'll be difficult again. Why can't you both –?

Scene 9

The CAPTAIN. BERTHA. LAURA.

LAURA. Oh, she's here. Now perhaps we can hear her opinion, since her fate is about to be decided.

CAPTAIN. The child can hardly be expected to hold an informed opinion on what a young girl ought to do with her life. We are at least partly qualified to judge, since we have seen a good many young girls grow up.

LAURA. But since we differ, let Bertha decide.

CAPTAIN. No! I permit no one to usurp my rights – neither woman nor child. Bertha, leave us.

BERTHA *goes.*

LAURA. You were afraid to let her speak, because you knew she'd agree with me.

CAPTAIN. I happen to know she wants to leave home. But I also know that you have the power to alter her will at your pleasure.

LAURA. Oh, am I so powerful?

CAPTAIN. Yes. You have a satanic genius for getting what you want. But that's always the way with people who aren't scrupulous about what means they use. How, for example, did you get rid of Dr. Norling, and find this new man?

LAURA. Well, how did I?

CAPTAIN. You insulted Norling, so that he went, and got your brother to fix this fellow's appointment.

LAURA. Well, that was very simple, wasn't it? And quite legal. Is Bertha to leave at once?

CAPTAIN. In a fortnight.

LAURA. Is that final?

CAPTAIN. Yes.

LAURA. Have you spoken to Bertha?

CAPTAIN. Yes.

LAURA. Then I shall have to stop it.

CAPTAIN. You can't.

LAURA. Can't? You think I'm prepared to let my daughter live with wicked people who'll tell her that everything I taught her is nonsense, so that she'll despise her mother for the rest of her life?

CAPTAIN. Do you think I am prepared to allow ignorant and conceited women to teach my daughter that her father is a charlatan?

LAURA. That should matter less to you.

CAPTAIN. Why?

LAURA. Because a mother is closer to her child. It has recently been proved that no one can be sure who is a child's father.

CAPTAIN. What has that to do with us?

LAURA. You can't be sure that you are Bertha's father.

CAPTAIN. I – can't be sure – !

LAURA. No. No one can be sure, so you can't.

CAPTAIN. Are you trying to be funny?

LAURA. I'm only repeating what you've taught me. Anyway, how do you know I haven't been unfaithful to you?

CAPTAIN. I could believe almost anything of you, but not that. Besides, if it were true you wouldn't talk about it.

LAURA. Suppose I were prepared for anything – anything – to be driven out, despised, anything – rather than lose my child? Suppose I am telling you the truth now, when I say to you: 'Bertha is my child, but not yours!' Suppose – !

CAPTAIN. Stop!

LAURA. Just suppose. Your power over her would be ended.

CAPTAIN. If you could prove I was not the father.

LAURA. That wouldn't be difficult. Would you like me to?

CAPTAIN. Stop it! At once!

LAURA. I'd only need to name the true father, and tell you the time and place. For instance – when was Bertha born? Three years after our marriage –

CAPTAIN. Stop it, or – !

LAURA. Or what? All right, I'll stop. But think carefully before you take any decision. And, above all, don't make yourself ridiculous.

CAPTAIN. God – I could almost weep – !

LAURA. Then you *will* be ridiculous.

CAPTAIN. But not you!

LAURA. No. Things have been arranged more wisely for us.

CAPTAIN. That is why one cannot fight with you.

LAURA. Why try to fight with an enemy who is so much stronger?

CAPTAIN. Stronger?

LAURA. Yes. It's strange, but I've never been able to look at a man without feeling that I am stronger than him.

CAPTAIN. Well, for once you're going to meet your match. And I'll see you never forget it.

LAURA. That'll be interesting.

NURSE (*enters*). Dinner's ready. Will you come and eat?

LAURA. Thank you.

The CAPTAIN *hesitates, then sits in a chair by the table, next to the sofa.*

LAURA. Aren't you going to eat?

CAPTAIN. No, thank you. I don't want anything.

LAURA. Are you sulking.?

CAPTAIN. No. I'm not hungry.

LAURA. Come along, or there'll be questions asked. Be good now. Oh, very well. If you won't, you'd better go on sitting there. (*Goes.*)

NURSE. Mr. Adolf! What is all this?

46

CAPTAIN. I don't know. Can you explain to me how it is that you women can treat an old man as though he was a child?

NURSE. Don't ask me. I suppose it's because, whether you're little boys or grown men, you're all born of woman.

CAPTAIN. But no woman is born of man. Yes, but I *am* Bertha's father! Tell me, Margaret! You do believe that? Don't you?

NURSE. Lord, what a child you are! Of course you're your own daughter's father. Come and eat now, and don't sit there sulking. There! There now, come along!

CAPTAIN (*gets up*). Get out, woman! Back to hell, you witches! (*Goes to the door leading to the hall.*) Svaerd! Svaerd!

BATMAN (*enters*). Sir?

CAPTAIN. Harness the sleigh! At once!

NURSE. Captain! Now, listen – !

CAPTAIN. Out, woman! At once!

NURSE. Lord help us, what's going to happen now?

CAPTAIN (*puts on his hat and makes ready to go out*). Don't expect me home before midnight! (*Goes.*)

NURSE. Blessed Jesus preserve us, how's this all going to end?

ACT TWO

As in Act One. The lamp is burning on the table. It is night.

Scene 1

The DOCTOR. LAURA.

DOCTOR. After my conversation with your husband, I am by no means convinced that your fears are justified. You made a mistake when you told me he had reached these surprising conclusions about other heavenly bodies by the use of a microscope. Now that I hear it was a spectroscope, he must not only be acquitted of any suspicion of derangement, but appears to have made a genuine contribution to science.

LAURA. But I never said that.

DOCTOR. Madam, I took notes of our conversation, and I remember I questioned you on this very point, because I thought I must have misheard you. One must be most meticulous in such accusations, for they could result in a man being certified as incapable of managing his affairs.

LAURA. Certified as incapable – ?

DOCTOR. Yes. Surely you know that a person who is *non compos* loses all his civic and family rights?

LAURA. No, I didn't know that.

DOCTOR. There is one further point on which I feel uneasy. He told me that his letters to booksellers had remained unanswered. Permit me to ask whether you, no doubt from the best of motives, perhaps intercepted them?

LAURA. Yes, I did. I had to protect my family. I couldn't let him ruin us all without doing something.

DOCTOR. Forgive me, but I don't think you can have realized the consequences of such an action. If he finds that you have

48

been secretly interfering in his affairs, his suspicions will be confirmed, and they will grow like an avalanche. Besides, by doing this you have fettered his will and further inflamed his impatience. You must have felt yourself how agonizing it is when one's most fervent wishes are obstructed, and one's wings are clipped.

LAURA. Yes, I have.

DCOTOR. Well, then, judge how he must feel.

LAURA (*rises*). It's midnight, and he hasn't come home. We must be ready for the worst.

DOCTOR. But, tell me, Mrs. Lassen, what happened this evening after I left? I must know everything.

LAURA. Oh, he raved and said the most extraordinary things. Can you imagine – he asked if he really was the father of his child!

DOCTOR. How very strange! Where did he get that idea?

LAURA. I can't imagine. Unless – well, he'd been questioning one of the men about who was the father to some baby, and when I took the girl's side he became furious and said no one could know for sure who was any child's father. God knows I tried my best to calm him, but now I don't see that there's anything more we can do. (*Weeps.*)

DOCTOR. This mustn't be allowed to continue. Something must be done. But we mustn't arouse his suspicions. Tell me, has the Captain had such delusions before?

LAURA. It was the same six years ago. Then he actually admitted in a letter to the doctor that he feared for his own sanity.

DOCTOR. Dear me! This obviously springs from something very deep-rooted. I mustn't inquire into the sacred secrets of family life, etcetera; I must confine myself to visible symptoms. What is done cannot, alas, be undone; but some steps should have been taken earlier. Where do you suppose he is now?

LAURA. I can't imagine. He gets such wild ideas nowadays.

DOCTOR. Would you like me to wait till he comes back? I could say that your mother has been feeling poorly, and that I have been attending her. That would lull his suspicions.

LAURA. Yes, do that. Oh, please don't leave us! If you knew how worried I am! But wouldn't it be better to tell him straight out what you think about his condition?

DOCTOR. No, one must never do that with people who are mentally sick. Certainly not until they raise the subject themselves, and then only under certain circumstances. It all depends how things develop. But we mustn't sit in here. Perhaps I should go next door? Then he won't suspect anything.

LAURA. Yes, that's a good idea. Margaret can sit in here. She always stays up when he goes out, and she's the only one who can do anything with him. (*Goes to the door, left.*) Margaret! Margaret!

NURSE. What is it, madam? Is the master home?

LAURA. No, but I want you to sit here and wait for him. When he comes, tell him that my mother is ill and the doctor has come to visit her.

NURSE. Very well. You leave it to me.

LAURA (*opens the door, left*). Will you come in here, Doctor?

DOCTOR. Thank you.

Scene 2

NURSE (*at the table; picks up a prayerbook and her spectacles*). Yes, yes! Yes, yes!

Reads half to herself.

> A wretched and a grievous thing
> Is life, this vale of suffering.
> Death's angel hovers ever near,
> And whispers into each man's ear:
> 'All's vanity! All's vanity!'
> Yes, yes! Yes, yes!
>
> All things that live upon the earth
> Fall to the ground before his wrath;
> And only sorrow's ghost survives

To carve above the green-dug grave:
'All's vanity! All's vanity!'
Yes, yes! Yes, yes!

BERTHA (*enters with a tray of coffee and a piece of embroidery.
She whispers*). Margaret, can I sit with you? It's so horrid up
there.

NURSE. Heaven preserve us! Are you still up?

BERTHA. I've got to finish father's Christmas present, you see.
And, look! I've something for you!

NURSE. But, my dear Miss Bertha, you can't do this. You've
got to get up in the morning, and it's past midnight.

BERTHA. Well, what of it? I daren't sit up there alone. I'm
sure there are ghosts about.

NURSE. You see! What did I say? Yes, mark my word, there's
no good angel guarding this house. What kind of thing did
you hear?

BERTHA. Oh, do you know – I heard someone singing up in the
attic!

NURSE. In the attic! At this time of night!

BERTHA. Yes. It was a sad song – so sad – I've never heard
anything like it before. And it sounded as if it came from the
cupboard where the cradle is – you know, on the left –

NURSE. Oi, oi, oi! And with such a storm blowing tonight!
I'm frightened it'll bring the chimney-pots down. 'What is
this life but toil and care? A moment's hope, then long
despair!' Well, my dear child, may God grant us a happy
Christmas!

BERTHA. Margaret, it is true father is ill?

NURSE. I'm afraid so.

BERTHA. Then we won't be able to have Christmas. But how
can we be up, if he's ill?

NURSE. Well, my child, with his kind of illness you can stay up.
Ssh! There's someone on the steps. Go to bed, now, and
hide this (*indicates the coffee tray*), or the master'll be angry.

BERTHA (*goes out with the tray*). Good night, Margaret.

NURSE. Good night, my child. God bless you.

Scene 3

The NURSE. *The* CAPTAIN.

CAPTAIN (*takes off his greatcoat*). Are you still up ? Go to bed!
NURSE. I only wanted to wait till you –

The CAPTAIN *lights a candle, opens the secretaire, sits down at it immediately and takes from his pocket letters and newspapers.*

NURSE. Mr. Adolf!
CAPTAIN. What do you want ?
NURSE. The old lady's sick. And the doctor's here.
CAPTAIN. Is it dangerous ?
NURSE. No, I don't think so. Just a chill.
CAPTAIN (*gets up*). Who was the father of your child, Margaret ?
NURSE. Oh, I've told you so many times. That good-for-nothing Johansson.
CAPTAIN. Are you sure it was he ?
NURSE. Don't be silly. Of course I'm sure. He was the only one.
CAPTAIN. Yes, but was *he* sure he was the only one ? No, he couldn't be. But you could be. There's a difference, you see.
NURSE. I can't see the difference.
CAPTAIN. No, you can't see it, but the difference is there. (*Turns the pages of a photograph album on the table.*) Do you think Bertha is like me ? (*Looks at a portrait in the album.*)
NURSE. You're as alike as two berries on a bough.
CAPTAIN. Did Johansson admit he was the father ?
NURSE. He had to.
CAPTAIN. It's horrible – ! There's the doctor.

Scene 4

The CAPTAIN. *The* NURSE. *The* DOCTOR.

CAPTAIN. Good evening, Doctor. How is my mother-in-law?

DOCTOR. Oh, it's nothing serious. She's just sprained her left foot slightly.

CAPTAIN. I thought Margaret said she had a chill. There seem to be two rival diagnoses. Go to bed, Margaret.

The NURSE *goes. Pause.*

CAPTAIN. Please sit down, Doctor.

DOCTOR (*sits*). Thank you.

CAPTAIN. Is it true that if you cross a zebra with a horse, you get striped foals?

DOCTOR (*surprised*). That is perfectly correct.

CAPTAIN. Is it also true that if you cross the same mare with an ordinary stallion, the foals may continue to be striped?

DOCTOR. Yes, that is also true.

CAPTAIN. Then, in certain circumstances a brown stallion can sire a striped foal, and vice versa?

DOCTOR. Apparently.

CAPTAIN. *Ergo*, the resemblance that a child bears to its father means nothing?

DOCTOR. Oh –

CAPTAIN. *Ergo*, it can never be proved who is a child's father?

DOCTOR. Er – hm – !

CAPTAIN. You are a widower and have had children?

DOCTOR. Er – yes –

CAPTAIN. Didn't you sometimes feel that your position was ridiculous? I know nothing so ludicrous as to see a father walking with his child on the street, or hear a father talking about his children. 'My wife's children', he should say. Did you never feel the falseness of your position, had you never any pinpricks of doubt? I don't use the word suspicion, for as a gentleman I assume that your wife was above suspicion.

DOCTOR. Indeed I did not! Has not Goethe written: 'A man must take his children on trust'?

CAPTAIN. Trust, where a woman's concerned? That's risky!

DOCTOR. But there are so many kinds of women.

CAPTAIN. Recent research has proved that there is only one kind. When I was young, I was strong and, I flatter myself, handsome. Let me quote you just two incidents which subsequently caused me to ponder. Once I was travelling on a steamer. I was sitting with some friends in the lounge. The young waitress came and sat herself opposite me in tears, and told me that her fiancé had been drowned. I pitied her, and ordered some champagne. After the second glass, I touched her foot; after the fourth, her knee; and before morning, I had consoled her.

DOCTOR. That was just a fly in winter.

CAPTAIN. Now to my second; and this was a fly in summer. I was at Lysekil. There was a young wife there, with her children – but her husband was in town. She was religious, had very strict principles, read me moral lectures, preached sermons at me – was completely honourable, I still believe. I lent her a book, two books. When the time came for her to leave, strange to relate, she returned them. Three months later, I found in one of these books a visiting card bearing a pretty explicit declaration of love. It was innocent, as innocent as a declaration of love can be from a married woman to a stranger who has never made an advance to her. The moral? Never trust anyone too much!

DOCTOR. Nor too little!

CAPTAIN. Exactly; just so far and no further. But, you see, Doctor, that woman was so unconsciously mischievous that she told her husband she had developed a passion for me. That's just the danger, they don't realize their instinctive capacity for creating mischief. It's an extenuating circumstance, but it doesn't nullify their guilt, it merely lessens it.

DOCTOR. Captain, these are unhealthy thoughts. You should keep a watch on yourself –

CAPTAIN. You mustn't use that word, unhealthy. You see, all boilers explode when the manometer reaches breaking-point;

but they don't all have the same breaking-point – you understand? Still, you're here to keep an eye on me. If I were not
a man I would have the right to accuse – or, as the polite
phrase is, to lay a complaint. Then I might perhaps be able
to give you a complete diagnosis of my illness, and, what is
more, its history. But unfortunately, I am a man, and so I
can only, like a Roman, fold my arms across my breast and
hold my breath until I die. Good night.

DOCTOR. Captain! If you are ill, it cannot be any reflection on
your honour as a man to tell me the truth. I must hear both
sides.

CAPTAIN. I should have thought you'd had enough listening to
one.

DOCTOR. No, Captain. Do you know, when I sat in the theatre
the other evening and heard Mrs. Alving orating over her
dead husband, I thought to myself: 'What a damned shame
the fellow's dead and can't defend himself!'

CAPTAIN. If he'd been alive, do you think he'd have dared to
open his mouth? If any dead man rose from his grave, do
you think he'd be believed? Good night, Doctor. As you can
hear, I am perfectly calm, so you can sleep in peace.

DOCTOR. Good night, then, Captain. I cannot take any further
part in this matter.

CAPTAIN. Are we enemies?

DOCTOR. By no means. The pity is that we cannot be friends.
Good night. (*Goes.*)

CAPTAIN (*accompanies the* DOCTOR *to the door upstage. Then
he goes to the door left, and opens it slightly*). Come in. I heard
you listening.

Scene 5

LAURA *enters embarrassed. The* CAPTAIN *sits down at the
secretaire.*

CAPTAIN. It's late, but we must talk this matter out. Sit down!
(*Pause.*) This evening I went to the post office and collected

my letters. It is evident from them that you have been inter-
cepting both my outgoing and my incoming correspondence.
The resultant waste of time has virtually destroyed the value
of my researches.

LAURA. I was acting from kindness. You were neglecting your
duties for this work.

CAPTAIN. You were not acting from kindness. You feared that
some day I might win more honour through these researches
than through my military career, and you were determined
that I should not win any honour, because that would throw
into relief your insignificance. Now I have confiscated some
letters addressed to you.

LAURA. How noble of you.

CAPTAIN. I'm glad you appreciate my qualities. It is clear from
these letters that for some time you have been turning all my
former friends against me by spreading a rumour concerning
my sanity. And you've succeeded, for now hardly one of
them, from my commanding officer to my cook, regards me
as sane. The situation regarding my mental condition is as
follows. My brain is, as you know, unaffected, since I
can perform both my professional duties and my duties
as a father. I still have my emotions more or less under
control, and my will is, to date, fairly unimpaired, but
you have been chipping and chafing at it so that soon
the cogs will disengage and the wheels will start whirl-
ing backwards. I shall not appeal to your feelings, for
you have none – that is your strength. But I appeal to your
self-interest.

LAURA. Go on.

CAPTAIN. By your behaviour you have succeeded in filling my
mind with doubt, so that soon my judgement will be clouded
and my thoughts begin to wander. This is the approaching
dementia for which you have been waiting, and which may
come at any time. Now you must ask yourself the question:
is it not more to your interest that I should be well rather
than ill? Think carefully? If I break down, I shall lose my
job, and you will be without support. If I die, you will receive
the insurance on my life; but if I kill myself, you will get

nothing. So it is to your own interest that I should go on living.

LAURA. Is this a trap?

CAPTAIN. Yes. It is up to you whether you go round it or stick your neck in it.

LAURA. You say you'll kill yourself. You won't!

CAPTAIN. Are you sure? Do you think a man can live when he has nothing and no one to live for?

LAURA. Then you capitulate?

CAPTAIN. No. I propose an armistice.

LAURA. And your conditions?

CAPTAIN. That I retain my sanity. Free me from my doubts, and I will abandon the battle.

LAURA. What doubts?

CAPTAIN. About Bertha's parentage.

LAURA. Are there any doubts about that?

CAPTAIN. In my mind there are. You have awoken them.

LAURA. I?

CAPTAIN. Yes. You have dripped them into my ear like poison, and events have fostered their growth. Free me from my uncertainty, tell me straight out: 'It is so!' and already I forgive you.

LAURA. How can I confess to a crime I have not committed?

CAPTAIN. What does it matter? You know I shan't reveal it. Do you think a man goes around trumpeting his shame?

LAURA. If I say it isn't true, you won't be sure; but if I say it is, you will be. So you would rather it was true.

CAPTAIN. Yes. It's strange, but I suppose it's because the one cannot be proved, whereas the other can.

LAURA. Have you any grounds for your suspicions?

CAPTAIN. Yes and no.

LAURA. I suppose you'd like me to be guilty so that you could throw me out and keep the child to yourself. But you won't catch me with a trick like that.

CAPTAIN. Do you think I'd want to keep some other man's child if I knew you were guilty?

LAURA. I'm sure you wouldn't. And that's why I realize you

were lying just now when you said you already forgave me.

CAPTAIN (*gets up*). Laura, save me and my sanity. You don't understand what I'm saying. If the child is not mine, I have no rights over her, and want none – and that is all that *you* want. Isn't it? Or do you want something else too? Do you want to retain your power over the child, but to keep me here as the breadwinner?

LAURA. Power? Yes. What has this life-and-death struggle been for if not for power?

CAPTAIN. I do not believe in resurrection, and to me this child was my life hereafter. She was my idea of immortality – perhaps the only one that has any roots in reality. Take her away and you cut short my life.

LAURA. Why didn't we part while there was still time?

CAPTAIN. Because the child bound us together. But the bond became a chain. How did it become that? How? I've never thought about it, but now memories return, accusing, condemning. We had been married for two years, and had no children, you best know why. I fell ill, and lay near to death. In a lucid moment I hear voices from the drawing-room. It is you and the lawyer, talking about my money – I still had some then. He is explaining that you cannot inherit anything because we have no children, and he asks if you are pregnant. I didn't hear your reply. I got better, and we had a child. Who is the father?

LAURA. You!

CAPTAIN. No, it is not I! A crime lies buried here, and it's beginning to come to light. And what a hellish crime! You women were soft-hearted enough to free your black slaves, but you keep your white ones! I have worked and slaved for you, for your child, your mother, your servants. I have sacrificed my life and my career, I have undergone torture, scourging, sleeplessness, every kind of torment for you, my hair has turned grey, all so that you might live free from care and, when you grow old, enjoy new life through your child. All this I have borne without complaint, because I believed I was the father to this child. This is the most arrant form of theft, the most brutal slavery. I have served seventeen years of hard labour for a crime I did not commit. What can you give me in return?

LAURA. Now you really *are* mad.

CAPTAIN (*sits*). So you hope. And I have seen how you worked to hide your crime. I pitied you, because I didn't understand why you were sad. I often calmed your evil conscience, supposing that I was driving away some sick thought. I heard you cry aloud in your sleep, though I didn't want to listen. Now I remember – the night before last! It was Bertha's birthday. It was between two and three o'clock in the morning, and I was sitting up, reading. You screamed as though someone was trying to strangle you: 'Don't come, don't come!' I banged on the wall because – because I didn't want to hear any more. I have had my suspicions for a long time, but I didn't dare to hear them confirmed. I have suffered all this for you. What will you do for me?

LAURA. What can I do? I will swear by God and all that is sacred that you are Bertha's father.

CAPTAIN. What good will that do, when you have already said that a mother should commit any crime for the sake of her child? I implore you, by the memory of the past – I beg you, as a wounded man begs for mercy – tell me everything! Don't you see that I am as helpless as a child, can't you hear me crying for pity like a child crying to its mother, can't you forget that I am a man, a soldier who with a word can tame men and beasts? I ask only for the pity you would extend to a sick man, I lay down my power and cry for mercy – for my life.

LAURA (*has approached him and lays her hand on his forehead*). What! Man, you're crying!

CAPTAIN. Yes, I am crying, although I am a man. But has not a man eyes? Has not a man hands, limbs, heart, thoughts, passions? Does he not live by the same food, is he not wounded by the same weapons, warmed and cooled by the same summer and winter as a woman? If you prick us, do we not bleed? If you tickle us, do we not laugh? If you poison us, do we not die? Why should a man be forbidden to complain, or a soldier to weep? Because it is unmanly? Why is it unmanly?

LAURA. Weep, my child. Your mother is here to comfort you. Do you remember, it was as your second mother that I first entered into your life? Your big, strong body was afraid. You were a great child who had come too late into the world, or had come unwanted.

CAPTAIN. Yes, I suppose it was that. Father and mother had me against their will, and so I was born without a will. When you and I became one, I thought I was making myself whole; so I let you rule; and I who, in the barracks, among the soldiers, gave commands, was, with you, the one who obeyed. I grew up at your side, looked up to you as though to a superior being, listened to you as though I was your ignorant child.

LAURA. Yes, That's how it was, and I loved you as my child. But, do you know – I suppose you noticed it – every time your feelings towards me changed, and you approached me as my lover, I felt bashful, and your embrace was an ecstasy followed by pangs of conscience, as though my blood was ashamed. The mother became the mistress – ugh!

CAPTAIN. Yes. I saw it, but I didn't understand. I thought you despised my lack of masculinity, and I wanted to win you as a woman by being a man.

LAURA. That was your mistake. The mother was your friend, you see, but the woman was your enemy. Love between man and woman is war. And don't think I gave myself. I didn't give, I took – what I wanted to have. But you had the upper hand. I felt it, and I wanted to make you feel it.

CAPTAIN. No, you were always the one who had the upper hand. You could hypnotize me so that I neither saw nor heard, but only obeyed. You could give me a raw potato and make me think it was a peach, you could force me to admire your stupid whims as strokes of genius, you could have driven me to crime, yes, even to vice. For you lacked intelligence, and instead of following my advice you did as *you* wanted. But when, later, I awoke and looked about me and saw that my honour had been sullied, I wanted to wipe out the stain through a noble action, a brave deed, a discovery, or an honourable suicide. I wanted to go to war, but

I couldn't. It was then that I turned to science. Now, when I should stretch out my hand to receive the fruits of my labour, you chop off my arm. Now I am without honour, and I cannot go on living, for a man cannot live without honour.

LAURA. But a woman –

CAPTAIN. She has her children, but he has none. Yet you and I and all the other men and women in the world have gone on living, as innocently as children, living on fancies, ideals and illusions. And then we awoke. Yes, we awoke, but with our feet on the pillow, and he who woke us was himself a sleepwalker. When women grow old and cease to be women, they get beards on their chins. I wonder what men get when they grow old and cease to be men? We who greeted the dawn were no longer cocks but capons, and the hens answered our false call, so that when the sun should have risen we found ourselves sitting in moonlight among ruins, just like in the good old days. It had only been a fretful slumber, a wild dream. It was no awakening.

LAURA. You know, you ought to have been a poet.

CAPTAIN. Perhaps I ought.

LAURA. Well, I'm sleepy. If you've any more fantasies, keep them until morning.

CAPTAIN. One word more – and this isn't a fantasy. Do you hate me?

LAURA. Sometimes. When you are a man.

CAPTAIN. This is like racial hatred. If it is true that we are descended from the ape, it must have been from two different species. We aren't of the same blood, are we?

LAURA. What exactly are you trying to say?

CAPTAIN. I feel that, in this war, one of us must go under.

LAURA. Which one?

CAPTAIN. The weaker, of course.

LAURA. And the stronger is in the right?

CAPTAIN. Always. Because he is the one with power.

LAURA. Then I am in the right.

CAPTAIN. You think you have the power?

LAURA. Yes. And tomorrow I shall have it legally, when I have you certified.

CAPTAIN. Certified – ?

LAURA. Yes. And then I shall bring up the child myself, without having to listen to your visions.

CAPTAIN. And who will pay for the child's upbringing, when I am gone?

LAURA. Your pension.

CAPTAIN (*goes towards her threateningly*). How can you have me certified?

LAURA (*takes out a letter*). By this letter, an attested copy of which I have deposited with the authorities.

CAPTAIN. What letter?

LAURA (*moves backwards towards the door*). Yours! The one you wrote to the doctor telling him you were mad. (*The* CAPTAIN *looks at her dumbly*.) You have done your job as a father and a breadwinner. Now you are no longer needed, and you can go. You realize now that my intelligence is equal to my will, and since you are not prepared to stay and admit it, you can go!

The CAPTAIN *goes to the table, takes the burning lamp and throws it at* LAURA, *who has retreated through the door.*

ACT THREE

As in Act Two. But another lamp. The concealed door is barricaded with a chair.

Scene I

LAURA. *The* NURSE.

LAURA. Did he give you the keys?

NURSE. Give them to me? No, God forgive me, I took them out of his pocket. He'd left them in the coat he'd given Nöjd to brush.

LAURA. So Nöjd's on duty today, is he?

NURSE. Yes.

LAURA. Give them to me.

NURSE. But that's like stealing! Very well. Oh, listen to him up there, madam! To and fro, to and fro.

LAURA. Is the door safely locked?

NURSE. Yes. It's locked all right.

LAURA (*opens the secretaire and sits down to it*). You must try to control your feelings, Margaret. Our only hope is to remain calm. (*There is a knock on the door.*) Who's that?

NURSE (*opens the door to the hall*). It's Nöjd.

LAURA. Tell him to come in.

NÖJD (*enters*). A despatch from the Colonel!

LAURA. Give it to me. (*Reads.*) Nöjd, have you removed all the cartridges from the rifles and pouches?

NÖJD. As you ordered, ma'am.

LAURA. Then wait outside, while I answer the Colonel's letter.

NÖJD *goes.* LAURA *writes.*

NURSE. Madam, listen! Whatever can he be doing up there now?

63

LAURA. Be quiet while I'm writing.

The sound of sawing is heard.

NURSE (*half to herself*). Merciful Jesus preserve us all! Where's this going to end?

LAURA. There. Give this to Nöjd. My mother must know nothing of this. You hear!

The NURSE *goes to the door.* LAURA *opens the drawers of the secretaire and takes out some papers.*

Scene 2

LAURA. *The* PASTOR *takes a chair and sits beside* LAURA *at the secretaire.*

PASTOR. Good evening, sister. I've been away all day, as you know, so I couldn't come before. Well, this is a sad story.

LAURA. Yes, brother. It's the worst twenty-four hours I have ever experienced.

PASTOR. At all events I see no harm has come to you.

LAURA. No, thank God. But think what could have happened.

PASTOR. But tell me one thing. How did it begin? I've heard so many different versions.

LAURA. Well, it started with him talking some nonsense about not being Bertha's father, and ended with him throwing the burning lamp in my face.

PASTOR. But this is terrible! This is real insanity. What are we to do now?

LAURA. Try to prevent any further violence. The doctor has sent to the asylum for a straitjacket. I've written to the Colonel, and am trying to find out our financial situation. It's really disgraceful the way he's kept these accounts.

PASTOR. What a tragedy! Mind you, I've always feared something like this might happen! Fire and water, you know – they're bound to end in an explosion. What have you got in that drawer?

LAURA (*has pulled a drawer out of the desk*). Look. This is where he's been hiding everything.

PASTOR (*looks in the drawer*). Great heavens! Why, there's your doll! And your christening-cap – and Bertha's rattle – and your letters – and that locket – ! (*Touches his eyes with his handkerchief.*) He must have loved you very much, Laura, in spite of everything. I haven't kept things like that.

LAURA. I think he used to love me once. But time – time changes so many things.

PASTOR. What's that big paper? Why, it's a receipt for – for a grave! Well, better a grave than the asylum. Laura! Tell me – have you no share of the blame for all this?

LAURA. I? How could I be to blame for a man going mad?

PASTOR. Well, well. I shan't say anything. After all, blood is thicker than water.

LAURA. What do you mean by that?

PASTOR (*looks at her*). Now, listen, Laura.

LAURA. Yes?

PASTOR. Listen to me. You cannot deny that this fits in very nicely with your wish that you should bring up the child yourself.

LAURA. I don't understand.

PASTOR. I can't help but admire you!

LAURA. Me! Hm!

PASTOR. And I am to become the legal guardian of that free-thinker! Do you know, I have always regarded him as a tare among our wheat.

LAURA (*gives a short, stifled laugh. Then, suddenly serious*). And you dare say that to me – his wife?

PASTOR. You are too strong for me, Laura. Incredibly strong! Like a fox in a trap; you'd rather bite off your own leg than let yourself be caught. Like a master-thief; you scorn any accomplice, even your own conscience. Look at yourself in the mirror! You daren't!

LAURA. I never use mirrors.

PASTOR. No, you daren't. May I look at your hand? Not one spot of blood to betray you, no trace of the stealthy poison that lies hidden there! A little innocent murder, that the law cannot touch; an unconscious crime – unconscious? Brilliant, my dear, brilliant! But do you hear how he's working away

up there ? Take care ? If that man breaks loose, he'll cut you
to pieces!

LAURA. You talk too much. Have you a bad conscience?
Accuse me; if you can.

PASTOR. I cannot.

LAURA. You see! You can't; so I am innocent. You take care of
your ward, and I'll look after mine. Here comes the Doctor.

Scene 3

LAURA. *The* PASTOR. *The* DOCTOR.

LAURA (*rises*). Good evening, Doctor. At least you'll help me,
won't you ? Though I'm afraid there's not much anyone can
do. You hear how he's carrying on up there? Are you
convinced now?

DOCTOR. I am convinced that an act of violence has been
committed. The question is whether it was an outbreak of
anger or of madness.

PASTOR. Even if one ignores the actual assault, you must surely
admit that he suffers from fixed ideas.

DOCTOR. I think your ideas are even more fixed, Pastor.

PASTOR. If you are referring to my spiritual convictions –

DOCTOR. I wasn't. Madam, it is up to you whether you choose
to condemn your husband to imprisonment and a fine, or the
asylum. How would you describe the Captain's conduct?

LAURA. I can't answer that now.

DOCTOR. You mean you are not certain which course would
best serve the interests of your family ? Well, Pastor, what do
you say?

PASTOR. There'll be a scandal either way. I really don't know –

LAURA. If he only has to pay a fine, he may commit violence
again.

DOCTOR. And if he goes to prison he will soon be released.
Then I suppose we must regard it as best for all concerned
that he be treated as insane. Where is the nurse?

LAURA. Why do you ask?

DOCTOR. She must put the straitjacket on him, after I have talked with him and given her the signal. But not before! I have the thing outside. (*Goes into the hall and returns with a large package.*) Please ask the nurse to come in.

LAURA *rings.*

PASTOR. Dreadful, dreadful!

The NURSE *enters.*

DOCTOR (*unpacks the straitjacket*). You see this? When I decide that the moment has come, you must approach the Captain from behind and put this jacket on him, to prevent any further outbreaks. As you see, it has unusually long sleeves, to limit his movements. You must fasten these behind his back. These two straps go through these buckles here, and you can then tie them to the back of the chair, or the sofa, whichever is more convenient. Will you do this?

NURSE. No, Doctor, I can't. I can't!

LAURA. Why don't you do it yourself, Doctor?

DOCTOR. Because the patient mistrusts me. You, madam, would be the most proper person to do it; but I fear he mistrusts you too? (LAURA *grimaces.*) Perhaps you, Pastor – ?

PASTOR. No, no! I couldn't possibly!

Scene 4

LAURA. *The* PASTOR. *The* DOCTOR. *The* NURSE. NÖJD.

LAURA. Have you delivered the letter already?

NÖJD. Yes, madam.

DOCTOR. Ah, it's you, Nöjd. Now you know what's happened, don't you? The Captain is – mentally ill. You must help us to take care of the patient.

NÖJD. If there's anything I can do for the Captain, he knows I'll do it.

DOCTOR. Good. Now you must put this jacket on him –

NURSE. No, he mustn't touch him! He'd hurt him. No, I'll do it myself – so gently, gently. Let him wait outside, to help me if need be. He can do that.

There is a banging on the concealed door.

DOCTOR. There he is! Hide this under the shawl – yes, on that chair – and go outside, all of you. The Pastor and I will wait in here. That door won't hold for long. Get outside, now, all of you!

NURSE (*goes out left*). Blessed Jesus, help us!

LAURA *closes the secretaire and goes out.* NÖJD *exits upstage.*

Scene 5

The lock snaps, the chair crashes to the floor and the concealed door is flung open. The CAPTAIN *enters with a pile of books under his arm. The* DOCTOR. *The* PASTOR.

CAPTAIN (*puts the books on the table*). It's all here. I wasn't mad, you see. For example – *The Odyssey*, Book 1, line 215, page 6 in the Upsala translation. Telemachus speaking to Athene. 'Truly my mother asserts that he whom men call Odysseus is my father. But of this I cannot be sure, for no man knows for sure from whom he springs.' And he says this of Penelope, the chastest of women! Pretty, eh? And here we have the prophet Ezekiel. 'The fool saith: "See, here is my father!" But who can tell whose loins have begotten him?' That's clear enough. Now, what have we here? Mersläkow's *History of Russian Literature*. 'Alexander Pushkin, Russia's greatest poet, died more of grief at the widespread rumours of his wife's infidelity than of the bullet he received in the breast in a duel. On his deathbed, he swore that she was innocent.' Ass! Ass! How could he swear to *that*? You see! I read my books! Hullo, Jonas, you here? And the Doctor – yes, of course! Have they told you what I once said to an Englishwoman who complained that the Irish throw burning lamps

in their wives' faces? 'God, what women!' I said. 'Women?'
she lisped. 'Yes!' I replied. 'When things have reached the
pitch that a man who has loved and worshipped a woman
takes a burning lamp and throws it in her face, then you
know – !'

PASTOR. Then you know what?

CAPTAIN. Nothing! One never knows – one only believes – eh,
Jonas? One believes, and is saved. Yes, saved! But I know
that belief can damn a man! I know that.

DOCTOR. Captain!

CAPTAIN. Be quiet. I don't want to talk to you. I don't want
to hear you relaying everything they say in there like one of
these damned telephones! Yes, in there! Tell me, Jonas, do
you believe that you are your children's father? I remember
you used to have a tutor living with you whom people talked
about. Such beautiful eyes, they said he had.

PASTOR. Adolf! Take care, now – !

CAPTAIN. Put your hand under your hair and see if you can't
feel a couple of bumps there! I'm blessed if he hasn't gone
pale! Yes, yes, it was only talk – but, my God, how they
talked! But we're all objects of ridicule, we husbands. Isn't
that true, Doctor? How about your marriage couch? Didn't
you have a lieutenant billeted on you? Wait, now, let me
guess – wasn't he called – ? (*Whispers in the* DOCTOR'*s ear*.)
You see, he's gone pale too! Don't cry, now. She'd dead and
buried, and what's done can't be done again! I knew him,
though – now he's a – look at me, Doctor! – no, in the eyes!
– a major in the Dragoons. By God, I believe he's grown
horns too!

DOCTOR. Captain, can we please discuss something else?

CAPTAIN. You see! As soon as I mention the word horns, he
wants to talk about something else!

PASTOR. You realize, brother, that you are insane?

CAPTAIN. Yes, I know. But if I had the care of your antlered
heads for a week or two, I'd have you all behind bars too!
I am mad, but how did I become mad? It doesn't concern
you. It doesn't concern anyone. Let's talk about something
else. (*Takes the photograph album from the table*.) Dear God –

there is my child! Mine? But of course we can't be sure. Do you know what we have to do to be sure? First, marry to become socially respectable; then, soon afterwards, get divorced; and become lovers; and adopt the child. Then at least you can be sure it's your own adopted child. That's right, isn't it? But what good is all this to me? What good is anything to me now that you have taken away my hope of immortality, what good is my science and my philosophy now that I have nothing to live for, what use is my life to me now that I have no honour left? I grafted my right arm, half my brain, half my spinal cord on to another stem, because I believed they would unite into a single, more perfect tree, and then someone comes with a knife and cuts beneath the graft, so that now I am only half a tree – but the other tree goes on growing with my arm and half my brain, while I wither and die, for I gave the best parts of myself. Now I want to die! Do what you will with me! I no longer exist!

The DOCTOR *whispers to the* PASTOR. *They go into the room on the left. A few moments later,* BERTHA *enters.*

Scene 6

The CAPTAIN. BERTHA.

The CAPTAIN *sits huddled at the table.* BERTHA *goes over to him.*

BERTHA. Are you ill, father?

CAPTAIN (*looks up dully*). I?

BERTHA. Do you know what you've done? Do you know you threw a burning lamp at mother?

CAPTAIN. Did I?

BERTHA. Yes, you did! Think if you'd hurt her!

CAPTAIN. What would that have mattered?

BERTHA. You aren't my father if you can talk like that!

CAPTAIN. What's that you say? I'm not your father? How do

you know? Who has told you that? Who is your father, then? Who?

BERTHA. Well, not you, anyway.

CAPTAIN. Still not me! Who, then? Who? You seem well informed. Who's been priming you? Must I endure this, that my child comes and tells me to my face that I am not her father? But do you realize you're insulting your mother by saying that? Don't you understand that, if this is true, she is the one who has sinned?

BERTHA. Don't say anything against Mother, do you hear?

CAPTAIN. No, you stick together, you're all against me! And you've done so all the time!

BERTHA. Father!

CAPTAIN. Don't use that word again!

BERTHA. Father, father!

CAPTAIN (*draws her to him*). Bertha, my darling, my beloved child, of course you are my child! Yes, yes – it must be so – it *is* so. Those were just sick thoughts that came with the wind like pestilence and fever. Look at me, let me see my soul in your eyes! But I see her soul too! You have two souls, and you love me with one and hate me with the other! You must only love me! You must only have one soul, or you will never find peace, nor shall I. You must have only one thought, the child of my thought, and you shall have only one will, mine.

BERTHA. I don't want that! I want to be myself!

CAPTAIN. I won't let you do that! You see, I'm a cannibal, and I want to eat you. Your mother wanted to eat me, but she couldn't. I am Saturn, who ate his children because it had been prophesied that otherwise they would eat him. To eat or be eaten! That is the question. If I don't eat you, you will eat me, and you have already shown me your teeth. But don't be afraid, my beloved child. I won't hurt you. (*Goes to where the guns are on the wall and takes a revolver.*)

BERTHA (*tries to escape*). Help, mother, help! He wants to murder me!

NURSE (*enters*). Mr. Adolf, what is it?

CAPTAIN (*looks at the revolver*). Have you taken the cartridges?

NURSE. Yes, I've hidden them away. But sit down and calm yourself, and I'll bring them back to you.

She takes the CAPTAIN *by the arm and coaxes him down into the chair, where he remains sitting dully. Then she takes the strait-jacket and goes behind his chair.* BERTHA *tiptoes out left.*

NURSE. Do you remember, Mr. Adolf, when you were my dear little baby, how I used to tuck you up at night and say your prayers with you? And do you remember how I used to get up in the night to fetch you a drink? Do you remember how I lit the candle and told you pretty stories when you had bad dreams and couldn't sleep? Do you remember?

CAPTAIN. Go on talking, Margaret. It soothes my head so. Go on talking.

NURSE. All right, but you must listen, then. Do you remember how once you took the big carving knife and wanted to make boats, and how I came in and had to get the knife away from you by telling you a story? You were such a silly baby, so we had to tell you stories, because you thought we all wanted to hurt you. Give me that snake, I said, otherwise he'll bite you. And you let go of the knife. (*Takes the gun from the* CAPTAIN'*s hand.*) And then, when you had to get dressed and you didn't want to. Then I had to coax you and say I'd give you a gold coat and dress you like a prince. And I took your little body-garment, which was only of green wool, and held it in front of you and said: 'Put your arms in', and then I said: 'Sit still, now, and be a good boy while I button up the back!' (*She has got the straitjacket on him.*) And then I said: 'Stand up now, and walk nicely, so I can see how you look.' (*She leads him to the sofa.*) And then I said: 'Now it's time to go to bed.'

CAPTAIN. What's that, Nanny? Must I go to bed when I'm dressed? Damnation! What have you done to me? (*Tries to free himself.*) Oh, you damned woman! Who would have believed you could be so cunning? (*Lies down on the sofa.*) Caught, cropped, and cozened! And not to be allowed to die!

NURSE. Forgive me, Mr. Adolf, forgive me! But I wanted to stop you from killing the child!

CAPTAIN. Why didn't you let me kill the child? Life is a hell, and death a heaven, and the child belongs to heaven.

NURSE. What do you know about what comes after death?

CAPTAIN. That is all one does know. About life, one knows nothing. Oh, if one had only known from the beginning!

NURSE. Mr. Adolf! Humble your proud heart and pray to God for mercy. It still isn't too late. It wasn't too late for the robber on the cross, when our Saviour said to him: 'Today shalt thou be with me in Paradise.'

CAPTAIN. Are you croaking for carrion already, you old crow? (*The* NURSE *takes a prayer-book from her pocket. The* CAPTAIN *roars.*) Nöjd! Is Nöjd there?

NÖJD *enters.*

CAPTAIN. Throw this woman out! She wants to choke me to death with her prayer-book! Throw her out through the window, or up the chimney! Anywhere!

NÖJD (*looks at the* NURSE). God bless you, Captain, I can't do that! I just can't! If there were six men, yes, but a woman –

CAPTAIN. Aren't you stronger than a woman?

NÖJD. Of course I'm stronger, but there's something special about a woman that stops a man raising his hand against her.

CAPTAIN. What's special about them? Haven't they raised their hands against me?

NÖJD. Yes, but I can't, Captain! It's just as though you was to ask me to strike the Pastor. It's something that's in a man's blood, like religion. I can't!

Scene 7

As before. LAURA *gestures to* NÖJD *to go.*

CAPTAIN. Omphale! Omphale! Now you play with the club while Hercules winds your wool!

LAURA (*comes over to the sofa*). Adolf! Look at me! Do you think I am your enemy?

CAPTAIN. Yes, I do. I think you are all my enemies. My mother was my enemy. She didn't want to bring me into the world because my birth would cause her pain. She robbed my first embryo of its nourishment, so that I was born half-crippled. My sister was my enemy, when she taught me that I was her inferior. The first woman I kissed was my enemy – she gave me ten years of disease in return for the love I gave her. My daughter became my enemy, when you forced her to choose between you and me. And you, my wife, you were my mortal enemy, for you didn't let go of me until there was no life left in me.

LAURA. I don't know that I ever planned, or intended, what you think I have done. There may have been in me a vague desire to be rid of you, because you were an obstacle in my path; but if you see a plan in the way I have acted, then perhaps there was one, though I wasn't aware of it. I didn't plot any of this – it just glided forward on rails which you laid yourself – and before God and my conscience, I feel that I am innocent, even if I am not. Your presence has been like a stone on my heart, pressing and pressing until my heart rebelled against its suffocating weight. This is the truth, and if I have unintentionally hurt you, I ask your forgiveness.

CAPTAIN. That all sounds plausible. But how does it help me? And who is to blame? Perhaps our idea of marriage is to blame. In the old days, one married a wife; now one forms a partnership with a business woman, or moves in with a friend. And then one beds the partner, or defiles the friend. What became of love – healthy, sensuous love? It died, starved. And what is the offspring of this broker's-love, a blank cheque drawn on a bankrupt account? Who will honour it when the crash comes? Who is the father of our child?

LAURA. Those suspicions of yours about the child are completely unfounded.

CAPTAIN. That's just what's so horrible. If they were real, at least one would have something to grip on, something to cling to. Now there are only shadows, hiding in the bushes and poking out their heads to laugh – it's like fighting with air, a mock battle with blank cartridges. A real betrayal would have acted as a challenge, roused my soul to action. But now my thoughts dissolve in twilight, my brain grinds emptiness until it catches fire! Give me a pillow under my head! And put something over me, I'm cold. I'm so terribly cold!

LAURA *takes her shawl and spreads it over him. The* NURSE *goes out to fetch a pillow.*

LAURA. Give me your hand, friend.

CAPTAIN. My hand! Which you have tied behind my back? Omphale! Omphale! But I feel your soft shawl against my mouth. It's warm and smooth like your arm, and it smells of vanilla, as your hair did when you were young. Laura – when you were young – and we walked in the birch woods among the primroses – and thrushes sang! Beautiful, beautiful! How beautiful life was! And now it has become like this. You didn't want it to be like this, I didn't want it, and yet it happened. Who rules our lives?

LAURA. God alone rules –

CAPTAIN. The God of battle, then! Or the goddess, nowadays! Take away this cat that's lying on me! Take it away! (*The* NURSE *enters with the pillow and removes the shawl.*) Give me my tunic. Put it over me! (*The* NURSE *takes his military tunic from the clothes-hanger and drapes it over him.*) Ah, my brave lion's skin, that you would take from me! Omphale! Omphale! O cunning woman, who so loved peace that you discovered the art of disarming men! Awake, Hercules, before they take your club from you! You would rob us of our armour and have us believe that it is only tinsel. No, it was iron before it became tinsel. In the old days it was the smith who forged the soldier's tunic; now it is the seamstress. Omphale! Omphale! Strength has been vanquished by craft and weakness! Curse you, damned woman, and all your sex! (*Raises himself to spit, but falls back on the couch.*) What kind of a pillow have you given me, Margaret? It's so hard, and

so cold, so cold! Come and sit beside me here, on the chair,
That's right. May I rest my head in your lap? So. That's
warm! Bend over so that I can feel your breast. Oh, it is
sweet to sleep at a woman's breast, whether a mother's or a
mistress's, but sweetest at a mother's!

LAURA. Do you want to see your child, Adolf? Speak!

CAPTAIN. My child? A man has no children. Only women
have children, and so the future belongs to them, while we
die childless. Gentle Jesus, meek and mild, look upon this
little child – '

NURSE. Listen! He's praying to God!

CAPTAIN. No, to you, to send me to sleep. I'm so tired, so
tired. Good night, Margaret. Blessed be thou amongst
women –

He raises himself, but falls with a cry in the NURSE's *lap.*

Scene 8

LAURA *goes left, and calls the* DOCTOR, *who enters with the*
PASTOR.

LAURA. Help us, Doctor, if it isn't too late. Look, he's stopped
breathing!

DOCTOR (*takes the* CAPTAIN's *pulse*). He has had a stroke.

PASTOR. Is he dead?

DOCTOR. No. He may still awake, and live. But to what he
will awake, we do not know.

PASTOR. 'Once to die, but after this the judgement – '

DOCTOR. We must not judge or accuse him. You, who believe
that there is a God who rules men's destinies, must plead
this man's cause before the bar of Heaven.

NURSE. Oh, Pastor, he prayed to God in his last moment!

PASTOR (*to* LAURA). Is this true?

LAURA. It is true.

DOCTOR. Then my art is useless. Now you must try yours,
Pastor.

LAURA. Is that all you have to say at this death-bed, Doctor?

DOCTOR. That is all. My knowledge ends here. He who knows more, let him speak.

BERTHA (*enters left and runs to her mother*). Mother, mother!

LAURA. My child! *My* child!

PASTOR. Amen!

Miss Julie

A NATURALISTIC TRAGEDY
(1888)

Introduction to
Miss Julie

Strindberg wrote *Miss Julie* in July-August 1888 at the age of thirty-nine. He completed it, as he had *The Father*, in about a fortnight.

After coming to Denmark the previous November for the première of *The Father*, he had settled with his wife and three children in the village of Lyngby not far from Copenhagen. There they had leased rooms in an old castle belonging to an eccentric lady, aged around forty, who called herself the Countess Frankenau, though she was not in fact of noble birth. Her estate was managed by her bailiff Ludvig Hansen, a fellow of gipsy-like appearance with whom the Countess appeared to be having an affair. Hansen at first got on well with Strindberg; he shared the latter's interest in hypnotism, and gave him a demonstration of the art. Years later it transpired that Hansen was in fact not the Countess's lover but her ~~. brother, being the illegitimate son of her late father, and that they had kept this matter secret out of respect to the dead man's memory. But Strindberg did not know this at the time, and their supposed relationship formed one of the starting-points of *Miss Julie*.

Another starting-point for the play lay in Strindberg's old feeling of social inferiority towards his wife. Siri, when he first met her, had been a baroness. He, as he could never forget, was the son of a servant-girl, and all his life he retained a sense of resentment against people with an upper-class background. He was to use the valet, Jean, as a mouthpiece for this resentment.

Shortly after Strindberg had completed *The Father* the previous year, André Antoine, an employee in a Paris gas company, had started an experimental theatre in the Place Pigalle of exactly the kind of which Strindberg had long been dreaming. 'In view of the hoped-for generation of new playwrights', Antoine had declared, 'there will be needed a new generation of actors . . . The actor will no longer "speak his lines" in the classic manner; he will say them naturally, which is just as difficult to learn. . . . Purely mechanical movements, vocal effects, irrational and superfluous gestures will be banished. Dramatic action will be simplified by a return to reality and natural gestures. The old stagy attitudes will be replaced by effects produced only by the voice. Feelings will be expressed by familiar and real accessories; a pencil turned round, a cup overturned, will be as significant and have an effect as intense on the mind of the spectator as the grandiloquent exaggerations of the romantic drama. Is it necessary to note that this apparent revolution is nothing but a return to the great traditions, and that the most famous actors of the French stage got their finest effects from simple means? Has not Salvini moved us deeply by his sobriety of gesture? . . . Did not Molière himself, in two or three instances, take care to affirm the necessity of "acting as one speaks"?'

Strindberg had sent Antoine a French translation of *The Father*, and Antoine was astute enough to perceive its merits. He wrote enthusiastically to Strindberg telling him that he would have produced it immediately but for the fact that he had committed himself to a production of Ibsen's *Ghosts*, and promising that he would try to present it in the near future. This encouragement acted as a considerable stimulus to Strindberg to continue with the kind of half-length, one-set play of which *The Father* had been an example. Moreover, he had himself for some time been interested in the possibility of starting just such an experimental theatre in Scandinavia, and Antoine's success caused him to renew his efforts. On 3 June 1887 he sent a lengthy prospectus to the Swedish actor August Lindberg, who had played a leading role in the championing of Ibsen's works and had, in 1883, been the first European to dare to produce *Ghosts*. Strindberg's theatre was to be a travelling one. 'Only plays by August Sg. are to be acted', he wrote, with characteristic arrogance, 'and none of his old ones. I will write plays which will obviate the need for carrying round costumes, sets and properties. . . . There need never be any shortage of material, for I can write a one-act play in two days.'

Antoine's ideas and the success of his theatre exercised an important influence on Strindberg at this period; not because they were new to him, but because they confirmed what he already believed. Strindberg's own preface to *Miss Julie* echoes many of Antoine's sentiments. His hope that he might some-time 'see the full back of an actor throughout an important scene' is a reference to Antoine's already famous habit of turn-ing his back on the audience for long periods; the Théâtre Libre had, indeed, acquired the nickname of 'Antoine's Back'. (It was facetiously suggested that a rich uncle had threatened to cut him off if he ever showed his face on the stage.)

Another, though perhaps more indirect influence upon Strindberg at the time he was writing *Miss Julie* was Friedrich Nietzsche, to whose writings Georg Brandes had introduced him that summer. 'Buy a modern German philosopher called *Nietzsche*, about whom G.B. has been lecturing,' he wrote to Verner von Heidenstam on 17 May 1888, 'You will find every-thing worth reading there! Don't deny yourself this pleasure! N. is a poet too.' On 4 September he told Edvard Brandes: 'My spiritual uterus has found a tremendous fertilizer in Fried-rich Nietzsche, so that I feel like a dog about to litter! He is the man for me!' He was much attracted by Nietzsche's theory of the Superman, which seemed to him to offer some consolation against the impending domination of the world by women; here at last was a fellow spirit to support him against Ibsen, whose championship of the female sex Strindberg abominated. Later that year he wrote four letters to Nietzsche, three in French and one in an eccentric mixture of Greek and Latin. 'Je termine toutes mes lettres à mes amis: lisez Nietzsche!' he assured him in December. 'C'est mon *Carthago est delenda*!'

On 10 August 1888 he posted *Miss Julie* triumphantly to his Stockholm publisher, Karl Otto Bonnier. 'I take the liberty', he wrote, 'of hereby offering you the first naturalistic tragedy of the Swedish drama, and I beg you not to reject it without serious thought, or you will later regret it, for, as the German says "Ceci datera!" = this play will be remembered in history. ... P.S. *Miss Julie* is the first of a forthcoming series of natural-istic tragedies.' Eleven days later, having received no reply, he wrote again to Bonnier, telling him that Antoine was planning to stage *The Father*, and adding that 'in a week I shall be sending you a new naturalistic tragedy, even better than *Miss Julie* with three characters, a table and two chairs, and no sunrise!' This was a reference to *Creditors*, which he had already begun.

But Bonnier had already written to Strindberg the previous day rejecting *Miss Julie*, and their letters crossed. 'It is much too "risky"', Bonnier explained, 'much too "naturalistic" for us. We therefore dare not publish the play, as likewise I fear you will find difficulty in getting it produced.' A descendant of Bonnier has described this decision as the most unfortunate ever perpetrated by that distinguished house; but Karl Otto Bonnier was right in his final prognostication, for it was to be sixteen years before *Miss Julie* was performed in Sweden.

Strindberg accordingly offered the play to another publisher, Joseph Seligmann, who a decade earlier had published *The Red Room*, Strindberg's autobiographical account of life among the young artists and writers of Stockholm. 'It is nearly ten years', Strindberg wrote to him on 22 August 1888, 'since the first Swedish naturalistic novel appeared under your imprint, with the consequences that we know. Today I send for your perusal the first Swedish naturalistic drama, written as I think it should be, for the reasons I have given in the foreword.'

Seligmann accepted *Miss Julie*, on condition that he was allowed to make certain amendments. Strindberg had by now been thrown out of the castle at Lyngby after a row with his gipsy friend, and must have been feeling somewhat desperate. He therefore agreed to Seligmann's conditions, and for many years, until Alf Sjöberg's Stockholm production in 1949 based on the original manuscript, this slightly bowdlerized version was the only one used even, apparently, for the première in Denmark.

Despite this precaution, *Miss Julie* was widely attacked on publication for its immorality, its assailants including, rather surprisingly, Bjørnstjerne Bjørnson. However, that winter, with the help of Hans Riber Hunderup (who had produced and played *The Father*) and others, Strindberg at last succeeded in fulfilling his old ideal of founding a Scandinavian experimental theatre.[1] On 17 November 1888 he inserted an advertisement in the Danish newspaper *Politiken*:

'Since I intend at the earliest opportunity to open a Scandinavian Experimental Theatre on the pattern of the Théâtre Libre in Paris, I hereby announce that I invite plays of whatever kind to be sent to me for reading. Preferably they should have a contemporary setting, be of not too great a length, and not require elaborate machinery or a large cast.'

They acquired the little Dagmar Theatre in Copenhagen, and planned to open it in the beginning of January. Although the advertisement elicited no very exciting contributions, they had enough plays to make a start, for by the end of the year, in the five months since he had completed *Miss Julie*, Strindberg had written four more short plays, *Creditors*, *The Stronger*, *Pariah* and *Simoom*. After several postponements for this reason and that, it was eventually decided to inaugurate the season on 2 March with a double bill consisting of *Miss Julie* and *Creditors*. But the day before the première was due to take place, police arrived at the theatre with the news that the Danish censor had, somewhat belatedly, decided to ban *Miss Julie*. Siri tried to get the censor to relent, but without success, and the theatre was forced to open a week later, on 9 March, with a triple bill of *Creditors*, *Pariah* and *The Stronger*.

Since the rehearsals of *Miss Julie* had reached so advanced a stage, Strindberg and his associates sought around desperately for some way of overcoming the censor's ban, and eventually hit on the idea of giving a private performance at the Copenhagen University Students' Union. On 14 March 1889 *Miss Julie* thus received its première before an audience of a hundred and fifty students, their friends, and a handful of critics. Siri played the title role, and the part of Jean was taken by a young Danish actor named Viggo Schiwe, whom Strindberg immediately suspected of having an affair with his wife. The scene at this first performance was described by the correspondent of the Swedish newspaper *Dagens Nyheter*:

---

[1] On 14 November 1888 – the anniversary, as Strindberg noted with gratification, of the first performance of *The Father*.

We find ourselves in a depressing little room on the first
floor of a building in Bath-house Street in Copenhagen. The
window-shutters are screwed shut, and only a single lamp
illuminates the stage in front of us. The room is packed, and
when our eyes have accustomed themselves to the relative
darkness, we are able to study the people sitting or standing
under the low ceiling. Most of them are students, only six
or seven are women, but not so few of the *coryphées* of
Copenhagen are seated in the front rows. But we search in
vain for August Strindberg, though it has been announced
that he is to attend the performance. . . .

In front of the chairs a long, blue, half-transparent curtain
hangs from ceiling to floor. The bottom of it is concealed by
a broad board, behind which are the footlights. A gas-light
shines through at one side (later in the evening it was to
serve as the setting sun).

'Nine o'clock' it said on the tickets, for which the students
have been fighting for two days. The academic quarter[1] has
already passed, the hall – if one can so describe this large
room – is more than full, and people are beginning to grow a
little impatient. Feet are stamped and a cry of 'Ring it up!'
is heard.

'Shut up those galleryites!' shouts a witty citizen to those
sitting behind him.

'Galleryite yourself!' is the retort, and the stamping of
feet continues until at length a few faint sounds of a teaspoon
being tapped against a toddy glass make themselves heard.
There is a deal of hushing, and then, after another teaspoon-
tap, the blue curtain is drawn aside. A deathly silence reigns
in the 'auditorium', where the heat begins to be oppressive.
The ceiling is not so high but that a man standing on his
chair might not touch it with his hand, and there is no
ventilation.

The play, as is known, takes place in a kitchen, and completely new décor has had to be bought for the evening's
performance. To our surprise, it resembles a real kitchen. A

[1] In Scandinavia, academic events, such as lectures, normally
begin fifteen minutes after the advertised time.

plate-rack, a kitchen table, a speaking tube to the floor above, a big stove with rows of copper pots above it – in short, everything is there, presenting the living image of a real kitchen.

From the little programme sheets which have been handed out we see that the title role is to be played by Fru Essen-Strindberg, Christine by Fru Pio and the servant Jean by Hr. Schiwe. As regards the first-named, her performance appears to be precisely opposed to what the author intended. She is too cold, much too cold, and one gets no impression at all of the kind of woman who would seduce a man like Jean. Hr. Schiwe hardly suggested a servant; his manner was much more that of a gentleman and a *viveur*. Fru Pio, however, spoke her lines excellently.

Although the play was performed before an audience almost exclusively male, the author had been compelled to accept several deletions. The promised midsummer romp by farm-hands and serving girls did not materialize; we merely heard a violin playing a dance.

And so, after rather a tame final scene, the curtain fell, or, more correctly, the sacking was pulled across the stage. There is resounding applause and the actors are called to take their bow.

Then we gather round the tables, and our theatrical evening ends like any student party.

The author himself, we are told, 'stood half-hidden behind a door, his face pale and twisted with jealousy'. He was convinced that Siri and Schiwe were having an affair.

The performance – not surprisingly, considering the inadequacy of the presentation – aroused no great enthusiasm, and it was three more years before *Miss Julie* was publicly staged, on 3 April 1892 in Berlin, at Otto Brahm's Freie Bühne. But there were such vehement public protests that even Brahm dared not continue with the play, which had to be removed from the repertory after a single performance. The following year, however, on 16 January 1893, André Antoine fulfilled Strindberg's hopes by presenting it at his Théâtre Libre – the first time a Swedish dramatist had been performed in Paris since a play by King Gustav III had been staged at the Comédie-Française in 1803. *Miss Julie* received a mixed reception from the audience and most of the critics were hostile; but Antoine was well satisfied with the result of the evening. '*Miss Julie* has created a tremendous sensation,' he noted. 'Everything gripped the audience – the subject, the *milieu*, this concentration into a single ninety-minute act of a plot that would suffice for a full-length play. Of course there were laughter and protests, but one found oneself in the presence of something quite new.'

After the turn of the century, the climate of taste had sufficiently mellowed for *Miss Julie* to be publicly presented in other countries. In 1902 it was performed in Stuttgart, in 1903 in Hamburg, and in 1904 the young Max Reinhardt produced it in Berlin. The same year, sixteen years after it had been written, *Miss Julie* was at last staged in Sweden, for a single, somewhat surreptitious performance at Upsala. In 1905 it was performed in New York in Russian, with Alla Nazimova; and in 1906 in St Petersburg. The same year August Falck junior toured a production round the Swedish provinces, bringing it in December to Stockholm, where it was a great success. In 1907 the play was presented at Strindberg's own Intimate Theatre in Stockholm, where it was performed, on and off, no less than 134 times. In 1908 Strindberg arranged a special performance for Bernard Shaw, who was on a visit to Stockholm, and watched it with him.[1]

Miss Julie first reached London in 1912, when Octavia

---

[1] This performance was witnessed only by Strindberg, Shaw and Mrs. Shaw. August Falck and Manda Björling, who played the leading roles, had to be summoned especially from the archipelago where they were holidaying; since it was some little time since they had last performed the play, they studied their parts on the boat in. This was, astonishingly, the first time Strindberg ever saw *Miss Julie* performed (although present on the occasion of the 1889 première in Copenhagen, he had refused to watch the play). He hated visiting the theatre and, though he sometimes came to rehearsals, he seldom witnessed an actual performance, even of his own works.

Kenmore presented it at the Little Theatre in the Adelphi; it was received with complete bewilderment. London has since (to 1990) seen sixteen revivals, notably those in 1965 at the Old Vic Theatre (Maggie Smith, Albert Finney; directed by Michael Elliott), 1971 by the Royal Shakespeare Company at the Place (Helen Mirren, Donal McCann; directed by Robin Phillips) and 1983 at the Lyric, Hammersmith, transferring to the Duke of York's (Cheryl Campbell, Stephen Rea; directed by Clare Davidson).

Miss Julie has been filmed no less than five times: in 1912 in Sweden, in 1922 in Germany (with Asta Nielsen and William Dieterle), in 1947 in Argentina, in 1951 again in Sweden and in 1973 in England (based on the Royal Shakespeare Company's stage production of 1971). The 1951 film was a memorable production by Alf Sjöberg, containing magnificent performances by Anita Björk and Ulf Palme, and deservedly won the Grand Prix at the Cannes Film Festival of that year. It is one of the best translations of a classic ever made for the screen.

Strindberg's Preface to Miss Julie

The theatre, and indeed art in general, has long seemed to me a *Biblia pauperum*, a Bible in pictures for the benefit of the illiterate; with the dramatist as a lay preacher hawking contemporary ideas in a popular form, popular enough for the middle classes, who comprise the bulk of playgoers, to be able to grasp without too much effort what the minority is arguing about. The theatre has always been a primary school for the young, the semi-educated, and women, all of whom retain the humble faculty of being able to deceive themselves and let themselves be deceived – in other words, to accept the illusion, and react to the suggestion, of the author. Nowadays the primitive process of intuition is giving way to reflection, investigation and analysis, and I feel that the theatre, like religion, is on the way to being discarded as a dying form which we lack the necessary conditions to enjoy. This hypothesis is evidenced by the theatrical crisis now dominating the whole of Europe; and, not least, by the fact that in those cultural strongholds which have nurtured the greatest thinkers of our age, namely England and Germany, the art of writing plays is, like most of the other fine arts, dead.

In other countries, men have tried to create a new drama by pouring new ideas into the old forms. But this has failed, partly because the new thinkers have not yet had time to become popularized and thus educate the public to understand the issues involved; partly because polemical differences have so inflamed emotions that dispassionate appreciation has become impossible – the cheers and whistles of the majority exercise a pressure that upsets one's instinctive reaction – and partly also because we have not succeeded in adapting the old form to the new content, so that the new wine has burst the old bottles.

In my previous plays, I have not tried to do anything new – for that one can never do – but merely to modernize the form so as to meet the demands which I supposed that the new men and women of today would make of this art. To this end I chose, or let myself be caught up by, a theme which may be said to lie outside current party conflicts. For the problem of social ascent and decline, of higher or lower, better or worse, man or woman, is, has been and will be of permanent interest. When I took this theme from an actual incident which I heard about some years ago, and which at the time made a deep impression on me, it seemed to me suitable matter for tragedy; for it is still tragic to see one on whom fortune has smiled go under, much more to see a line die out. But the time may come when we shall have become so developed and enlightened that we shall be able to observe with indifference the harsh, cynical and heartless drama that life presents – when we shall have discarded those inferior and unreliable thought-mechanisms called feelings, which will become superfluous and harmful once our powers of judgement reach maturity. The fact that the heroine arouses our sympathy is merely due to our weakness in not being able to resist a feeling of fear lest the same fate should befall us. Even so, the hyper-sensitive spectator may possibly even feel that sympathy is not enough, while the politically-minded will doubtless demand positive measures to remedy the evil – some kind of 'programme'. But there is no such thing as absolute evil, since the death of a family is good luck for some other family that will be able to take its place, and social change constitutes one of the main pleasures of life, happiness being dependent on comparison. As for the political planner, who wishes to remedy the regrettable fact that the bird of prey eats the dove, and the louse eats the bird of prey, I would ask him: 'Why should this state of affairs be remedied ?' Life is not so foolishly and mathematically arranged that the great always devour the small. It happens equally often that a bee kills a lion, or at any rate drives it mad.

If my tragedy makes a tragic impression on people, they have only themselves to blame. When we become as strong as the first French revolutionaries, we shall feel uninhibited pleasure and relief at seeing our national forests thinned out by the removal of decayed and superannuated trees which have too long obstructed the growth of others with an equal right to live and fertilize their age – a relief such as one feels when one sees an incurable invalid at last allowed to die.

Recently, people complained of my tragedy *The Father* that it was too tragic – as though tragedies ought to be jolly. One hears pretentious talk about 'the joy of life',[1] and theatrical managers feverishly commission farces, as though joy consisted in behaving idiotically and portraying the world as though it were peopled by lunatics with an insatiable passion for dancing. I find 'the joy of life' in life's cruel and mighty conflicts; I delight in knowledge and discovery. And that is why I have chosen a case that is unusual but from which one can learn much – an exception, if you like, but an important exception which proves the rule – though I dare say it will offend those people who love only what is commonplace. Another thing that will offend simple souls is the fact that the motivation of my play is not simple, and that life is seen from more than one viewpoint. An incident in real life (and this is quite a new discovery!) is usually the outcome of a whole series of deep-buried motives, but the spectator commonly settles for the one that he finds easiest to understand, or that he finds most flattering to his powers of judgement. Someone commits suicide. 'Bad business!', says the business man. 'Unrequited love!', say the ladies. 'Bodily illness!', says the invalid. 'Shattered hopes!', says the man who is a failure. But it may be that the motive lay quite elsewhere, or nowhere, and that the dead man concealed his true motive by suggesting another more likely to do credit to his memory!

I have suggested many possible motivations for Miss Julie's unhappy fate. The passionate character of her mother; the upbringing misguidedly inflicted on her by her father; her own character; and the suggestive effect of her fiancé upon her weak and degenerate brain. Also, more immediately, the festive atmosphere of Midsummer Night; her father's absence; her menstruation; her association with animals; the intoxicating

---

[1] 'The Joy of life' (*livsglæde*) is a key-phrase in Ibsen's *Ghosts*, published seven years before Strindberg wrote *Miss Julie*.

effect of the dance; the midsummer twilight; the powerfully aphrodisiac influence of the flowers; and, finally, the chance that drove these two people together into a private room – plus of course the passion of the sexually inflamed man.

I have therefore not suggested that the motivation was purely physiological, nor that it was exclusively psychological. I have not attributed her fate solely to her heritage, nor thrown the entire blame on to her menstruation, or her lack of morals. I have not set out to preach morality. This, in the absence of a priest, I have left to a cook.

This multiplicity of motives is, I like to think, typical of our times. And if others have done this before me, then I congratulate myself in not being alone in my belief in these 'paradoxes' (the word always used to describe new discoveries).

As regards characterization, I have made my protagonists somewhat lacking in 'character', for the following reasons:

The word 'character' has, over the years, frequently changed its meaning. Originally it meant the dominant feature in a person's psyche, and was synonymous with temperament. Then it became the middle-class euphemism for an automaton; so that an individual who had stopped developing, or who had mould-ed himself to a fixed role in life – in other words, stopped grow-ing – came to be called a 'character' – whereas the man who goes on developing, the skilful navigator of life's river, who does not sail with a fixed sheet but rides before the wind to luff again, was stigmatized as 'characterless' (in, of course, a deroga-tory sense) because he was too difficult to catch, classify and keep tabs on. This *bourgeois* conception of the immutability of the soul became transferred to the stage, which had always been *bourgeois*-dominated. A character, there, became a man fixed in a mould, who always appeared drunk, or comic, or pathetic, and to establish whom it was only necessary to equip with some physical defect, such as a club-foot, a wooden leg or a red nose, or else some oft-repeated phrase, such as 'Absolutely first-rate!', 'Barkis is willin'!'[1], etc. This over-simplified view of people we find even in the great Molière. Harpagon is a miser and nothing else, although he might have been both miserly and a

[1] Thus in the original; Strindberg knew his Dickens.

first-class financier, a loving father, a good citizen. And, what is worse, his 'defect' is in fact extremely advantageous to both his daughter and his son-in-law, who are his heirs and are thus the last people who ought to blame him if they have to wait a little before gathering the fruits of his parsimony. So I do not believe in 'theatrical characters'. And these summary judgements that authors pronounce upon people – 'He is stupid, he is brutal, he is jealous, he is mean', etc. – ought to be challenged by naturalists, who know how richly complex a human soul is, and who are aware that 'vice' has a reverse image not dissimilar to virtue.

Since they are modern characters, living in an age of transition more urgently hysterical at any rate than the age which preceded it, I have drawn my people as split and vacillating, a mixture of the old and the new. And I think it not improbable that modern ideas may, through the media of newspapers and conversation, have seeped down into the social stratum which exists below stairs.

My souls (or characters) are agglomerations of past and present cultures, scraps from books and newspapers, fragments of humanity, torn shreds of once-fine clothing that has become rags, in just the way that a human soul is patched together. I have also provided a little documentation of character development, by making the weaker repeat words stolen from the stronger, and permitting the characters to borrow 'ideas', or, as the modern phrase is, accept suggestions from each other.

Miss Julie is a modern character – not that the half-woman, the man-hater, has not existed in every age, but because, now that she has been discovered, she has stepped forward into the limelight and begun to make a noise. The half-woman is a type that pushes herself to the front, nowadays selling herself for power, honours, decorations and diplomas, as formerly she used to for money. She is synonymous with corruption. They are a poor species, for they do not last, but unfortunately they propagate their like by the wretchedness they cause; and degenerate men seem unconsciously to choose their mates from among them, so that their number is increased. They engender an indeterminate sex to whom life is a torture, but fortunately they go under, either because they cannot adapt themselves

95

to reality, or because their repressed instinct breaks out uncontrollably, or because their hopes of attaining equality with men are shattered. It is a tragic type, providing the spectacle of a desperate battle against Nature – and tragic also as a Romantic heritage now being dissipated by Naturalism, which thinks that the only good lies in happiness – and happiness is something that only a strong and hardy species can achieve.

But Miss Julie is also a relic of the old warrior nobility, which is now disappearing in favour of the new neurotic or intellectual nobility; a victim of the discord which a mother's 'crime' implanted in a family; a victim of the errors of her age, of circumstances, and of her own flawed constitution, all of which add up to the equivalent of the old concept of Destiny or the Universal Law. The naturalist has abolished guilt with God, but he cannot expunge the consequences of her action – punishment, and prison, or the fear of it – for the simple reason that, whether or not he acquits her, the consequences remain. One's injured fellow-beings are not as indulgent as outsiders who have not suffered can afford to be. Even if her father felt impelled to postpone the moment of Nemesis, vengeance would be taken on his daughter, as it is here, by that innate or acquired sense of honour which the upper classes inherit – from where? From barbarism, from their Aryan forefathers, from medieval chivalry. It is very beautiful, but nowadays it is fatal to the continuation of the species. It is the nobleman's *hara-kiri*, the Japanese law of inner conscience which commands a man to slit his stomach when another has insulted him, and which survives in a modified form in that ancient privilege of the nobility, the duel. Thus, the servant, Jean, lives; but Miss Julie cannot live without honour. The slave has this advantage over the knight, that he lacks the latter's fatal preoccupation with honour; but in all of us Aryans there is a little knight or Don Quixote who makes us sympathize with the man who kills himself because he has committed a dishonourable act and thereby lost his honour. We are aristocrats enough to be sad when we see the mighty fallen and stinking corpse-like on the garbage-heap – yes, even if the fallen should arise and make atonement by honourable action. The servant Jean is the type who founds a species; in him, we trace the process of differentiation. He was the son of a poor peasant, and has now educated himself to the point where he is a potential gentleman. He has proved a quick student, possesses finely developed senses (smell, taste, sight), and an eye for beauty. He has already risen in the world, and is strong enough not to worry about using other people's shoulders to climb on. He has already reacted against his fellow servants, whom he despises as representing the world which he has left behind him; he fears them and shrinks from them because they know his secrets, sniff out his intentions, envy his rise and hopefully await his fall. Hence his dual, uncrystallized character, wavering between sympathy for the upper class and hatred of those who constitute it. He is, as he himself says, an aristocrat; he has learned the secrets of good society, is polished but coarse underneath; he knows how to wear a tail-coat, but can offer us no guarantee that his body is clean beneath it.

He respects Miss Julie, but is afraid of Christine, because she knows his dangerous secrets; and he is sufficiently callous not to allow the events of the night to interfere with his future plans. With the brutality of a slave and the indifference of a tyrant he can look at blood without fainting and shake off misfortune. So he survives the battle unharmed, and will quite possibly end as an *hôtelier*; and even if he does not become a Rumanian count, his son will probably get to university and very likely end up on the bench.

Incidentally, the information he gives us about the lower classes' view of life as seen from below is by no means negligible – when, that is, he speaks the truth, which is not often, for his tendency is to say what is likely to prove to his own advantage rather than what is true. When Miss Julie throws out the suggestion that the lower classes find the pressure from above intolerable, Jean naturally agrees, because he wants to win her sympathy, but he immediately corrects himself when he sees the advantage of differentiating between himself and the mass.

Apart from the fact that Jean's star is rising, he has the whip-hand of Miss Julie simply because he is a man. Sexually he is an aristocrat by virtue of his masculine strength, his more finely developed senses and his ability to seize the initiative. His sense of inferiority arises chiefly from the social *milieu* in which he temporarily finds himself, and he will probably throw it off when he discards his livery.

His slave-mentality expresses itself in his respect for the Count (the boots) and in his religious superstition; but he respects the Count principally as the holder of the social position which he himself covets. And this respect remains even when he has won the daughter of the house and seen the emptiness of that pretty shell.

I do not think that any 'love relationship' in the higher sense can exist between two spirits of such unequal quality, and I have therefore made Miss Julie imagine herself to be in love so as to excuse her action and escape her feeling of guilt; and I make Jean fancy that he might be able to fall in love with her, provided he could improve his social standing. I think it is the same with love as with the hyacinth, which has to strike roots in darkness before it can produce a strong flower. With these two, it shoots up, flowers and goes to seed in a moment, and that is why it so quickly dies.

What of Christine? She is a female slave, utterly conventional, bound to her stove and stuffed full of religion and morality, which serve her as both blinkers and scapegoats. She goes to church in order to be able to shift the guilt of her domestic pilferings on to Jesus, and get herself recharged with innocence. She is a supporting character, and I have therefore deliberately portrayed her as I did the priest and the doctor in *The Father*; I wanted them to appear everyday human beings, as provincial priests and doctors usually are. And if these supporting characters seem somewhat abstract, that is because ordinary people are, to a certain degree, abstract in the performance of their daily work – conventional, and showing only one side of themselves – and as long as the spectator feels no need to see their other sides, my abstract portrayal of them will serve well enough.

Finally, the dialogue. Here I have somewhat broken with tradition by not making my characters catechists who sit asking stupid questions in order to evoke some witty retort. I have avoided the symmetrical, mathematically constructed dialogue of the type favoured in France, and have allowed their minds to work irregularly, as people's do in real life, when, in conversation, no subject is fully exhausted, but one mind discovers in another a cog which it has a chance to engage. Consequently, the dialogue, too, wanders, providing itself in the opening scenes with matter which is later taken up, worked upon, repeated, expanded and added to, like the theme in a musical composition.

The plot is, I fancy, passable enough, and since it really only concerns two persons I have confined myself to them, introducing but one minor character, a cook, and making the unhappy spirit of the father hover over and behind the whole of the action. I have done this because I believe that what most interests people today is the psychological process. Our prying minds are not content merely with seeing something happen – they must know why it happens. We want to see the wires, see the machinery, examine the box with the false bottom, finger the magic ring to find the join, look at the cards to see how they are marked.

In this context I have been mindful of the realistic novels of the Goncourt brothers, which have attracted me more than anything else in contemporary literature.

On the question of technique, I have, by way of experiment, eliminated all intervals. I have done this because I believe that our declining capacity for illusion is possibly affected by intervals, which give the spectator time to reflect and thereby withdraw from the suggestive influence of the author-hypnotist. My play will probably run for about one and a half hours, and if people can listen to a lecture, a sermon or a parliamentary debate for that length of time, I think they should be able to endure a play for ninety minutes. As long ago as 1872, in one of my first dramatic attempts, *The Outlaw*, I aimed at this concentrated form, though with little success. I originally plotted it in five acts, and had already completed it before I noticed how broken and restless was its effect. I burned it, and from the ashes arose a single, long, integrated act of some fifty printed pages, which played for a full hour. This form is by no means new, though it appears at present to be my monopoly, and perhaps, thanks to the changing laws of taste, it may prove appropriate to the spirit of our time. My ultimate hope would be to educate an audience to the point where they will be able to sit through a full evening in the theatre without an interval. But one would have to examine the matter first. Meanwhile, in order to provide short periods of rest for the audience and the actors, without allowing the former to escape from my word of illusion, I have used three art-forms all of which properly belong to the drama – namely, the monologue, mime, and ballet. These were originally a part of ancient tragedy, the monody having developed into the monologue and the Greek chorus into ballet.

The monologue is nowadays abominated by our realists as being contrary to reality, but if I motivate it I make it realistic, and can thus use it to advantage. It is after all realistic that a speaker should walk up and down alone in his room reading his speech aloud, that an actor should rehearse his part aloud, a servant-girl talk to her cat, a mother prattle to her child, an old maid jabber at her parrot, a sleeper talk in his sleep. And, to give the actor the chance for once to create for himself, and get off the author's leash, it is better that monologues should be implied rather than specified. For, since it matters little what one says in one's sleep, or to one's parrot or cat (for it does not influence the action), so a talented actor, attuned to the atmosphere and situation, may be able to improvise better than the author, who cannot calculate in advance how much needs to be said, or for how long the audience will accept the illusion.

As is known, the Italian theatre has, in certain instances, returned to improvisation and thereby created actors who themselves create, on the author's blueprint. This may well be a step forward, or even a new species of art, of which we shall be able to say that it is an art that engenders art.

Where a monologue would seem unrealistic, I have resorted to mime, which leaves the player even more freedom to create and so gain independent recognition. But in order not to make too great a demand upon the audience, I have allowed music, well motivated by the midsummer dance, to exercise its illusory power during the dumb play. Here I would ask the musical director to take care when choosing his pieces not to evoke an alien atmosphere by echoes from popular operettas or dance tunes, or folk melodies with specific associations.

The ballet which I have introduced must not be smudged into a so-called 'crowd scene', because crowd scenes are always badly acted, and a mob of buffoons would seize the chance to be clever and so destroy the illusion. Since simple people do not improvise when they wish to be spiteful, but use ready-to-hand material, I have not written new words for them but have borrowed a little-known song which I discovered myself in the country-side near Stockholm. The words are circumlocutory rather than direct, but that is as it should be, for the cunning (weakness) of servile people is not of the type that engages in direct assault. So there must be no chattering or clowning in what is, after all, a serious piece of action, no coarse sniggering in a situation which drives the nails into the coffin of a noble house.

As regards the décor, I have borrowed from the impressionist painters asymmetry and suggestion (i.e., the part rather than the whole), believing that I have thereby helped to further my illusion. The fact that one does not see the whole room and all the furniture leaves room for surmise – in other words, the audience's imagination is set in motion and completes its own picture. I have also profited by eliminating those tiresome exits through doors; for stage doors are made of canvas and flap at the slightest touch; they will not even allow an angry father to express his fury by stumping out after a bad dinner and slamming the door 'so that the whole house shakes'. (In the theatre, the door simply waves.) I have likewise confined myself to a single set, both to enable the characters to accustom themselves to their *milieu*, and to get away from the tradition of scenic luxury. But when one has only one set, one is entitled to demand that it be realistic – though nothing is more difficult than to make a room which looks like a room, however skilful the artist may be at creating fire-spouting volcanoes and waterfalls. Even if the walls have to be of canvas, it is surely time to stop painting them with shelves and kitchen utensils. We have so many other stage conventions in which we are expected to believe that we may as well avoid overstraining our imagination by asking it to believe in painted saucepans.

I have placed the rear wall and the table at an angle so that the actors shall be able to face each other and be seen in demi-profile when they sit opposite each other at the table. In a performance of the opera *Aïda* I once saw a backcloth at an angle which led one's eyes off into an unknown perspective: nor did it look as though it had been arranged thus simply out of a spirit of reaction against the boredom of straight lines.

Another perhaps not unnecessary innovation would be the removal of the footlights. This illumination from below is said to serve the purpose of making actors fatter in the face; but I would like to ask: 'Why should all actors be fat in the face?' Does not this under-lighting annihilate all subtle expressions in the lower half of the face, particularly around the mouth? Does it not falsify the shape of the nose, and throw shadows up over the eyes? Even if this were not so, one thing is certain: that pain is caused to the actors' eyes, so that any realistic expression is lost. For the footlights strike the retina on parts of it which are normally protected (except among sailors, who see the sun reflected from the water), so that one seldom sees any attempt at ocular expression other than fierce glares either to the side or up towards the gallery, when the whites of the eyes become visible. Perhaps this is also the cause of that tiresome habit, especially among actresses, of fluttering eyelashes. And when anyone on the stage wishes to speak with his eyes, he has no alternative but to look straight at the audience, thereby entering into direct contact with them outside the framework of the play – a bad habit which rightly or wrongly, is known as 'greeting one's friends'.

Would not side-lights of sufficient power (with reflectors, or some such device) endow the actor with this new resource, enabling him to reinforce his mime with his principal weapon of expression, the movement of his eyes?'

I have few illusions of being able to persuade the actor to play *to* the audience and not with them, though this would be desirable. I do not dream that I shall ever see the full back of an actor throughout the whole of an important scene, but I do

fervently wish that vital scenes should not be played opposite
the prompter's box as though they were duets milking applause.
I would have them played at whatever spot the situation might
demand. So no revolutions, but simply small modifications;
for to turn the stage into a room with the fourth wall missing,
so that some of the furniture would have its back to the
audience, would, I suppose, at this juncture, simply serve as a
distraction.

A word about make-up; which I dare not hope will be listened to by the ladies, who prefer beauty to truth. But the actor
might well ponder whether it is to his advantage to paint an
abstract character upon his face which will remain sitting there
like a mask. Imagine a gentleman dipping his finger into soot
and drawing a line of bad temper between his eyes, and suppose that, wearing this permanently fierce expression, he were
called upon to deliver a line smiling? How dreadful would be
the result! And how is this false forehead, smooth as a billiard
ball, to wrinkle when the old man gets really angry?

In a modern psychological drama, where the subtler reactions
should be mirrored in the face rather than in gesture and sound,
it would surely be best to experiment with strong side-lights on
a small stage and with the actor wearing no make-up, or at best
a minimum.

If we could then dispense with the visible orchestra, with
their distracting lampshades and faces turned towards the
audience; if we could have the stalls raised so that the spectator's sightline would be above the actors' knees; if we could
get rid of the side-boxes (my particular *bête noire*), with their
tittering diners and ladies nibbling at cold collations, and have
complete darkness in the auditorium during the performance,
and, first and foremost, a *small* stage and a *small* auditorium –
then perhaps a new drama might emerge, and the theatre might
once again become a place for educated people. While we await
such a theatre, one must write to create a stock of plays in
readiness for the repertoire that will, some day, be needed.

I have made an attempt! If it has failed, there will, I hope, be
time enough to make another!

Translated by Michael Meyer

Miss Julie

This translation of *Miss Julie* was presented by The National Theatre at the Chichester Festival on 27 July 1965, and subsequently at the Old Vic Theatre, London on 8 March 1966, both times with the following cast:

MISS JULIE	Maggie Smith
JEAN, her father's valet	Albert Finney
CHRISTINE, her father's cook	Jeanne Watts
OTHER SERVANTS	Chloe Ashcroft,

Elizabeth Burger, Kay Gallie, Jennie Heslewood, Caroline John, Carolyn Jones, Pauline Taylor, Michael Byrne, Alan Collins, Neil Fitzpatrick, John Hallam, Ron Pember, Edward Petherbridge, Ronald Pickup, David Ryall, John Savident

MUSICIANS	Sydney Bliss
	Pierre Tas
	Henry Krein

Designed by Richard Negri
Directed by Michael Elliott

On 27 October 1971 it was performed by the Royal Shakespeare Company at The Place, Euston Road. The cast was:

MISS JULIE	Helen Mirren
JEAN	Donal McCann
CHRISTINE	Heather Canning
OTHER SERVANTS	Mary Allen, Isla

Blair, Colin Edwynn, Michael Egan, Ron Forfar, Julian Glover, Patrick Godfrey, Edward Phillips, Holly Wilson

Designed by Daphne Dare
Directed by Robin Phillips

This production was subsequently filmed, with the same cast and director.

*only ½ of Kitchen shown the other ½
left to our imagination. Lilacs -
associated with sex
Attempt to make Kitchen look real*

Miss Julie

*Specific
stage setting*

A large kitchen, the roof and side walls of which are concealed by drapes and borders. The rear wall rises at an angle from the left; on it, to the left, are two shelves with utensils of copper, iron and pewter. The shelves are lined with scalloped paper. Over to the right we can see three-quarters of a big, arched exit porch, with twin glass doors, through which can be seen a fountain with a statue of Cupid, lilac bushes in bloom, and tall Lombardy poplars. On the left of the stage is visible the corner of a big tiled stove, with a section of an overhead hood to draw away fumes. To the right, one end of the kitchen table, of white pine, with some chairs. The stove is decorated with birch-leaves; the floor is strewn with juniper twigs. On the end of the table is a big Japanese spice-jar containing flowering lilacs. An ice-box, a scullery table, a si   above the door is a big old-fashioned bell, of the alarm type. To the left of this emerges a speaking-tube.

OF FOOTLIGHTS 2 B USED.   *Real*

CHRISTINE *is standing at the stove, frying in a pan. She is dressed in a light cotton dress, with apron.* JEAN *enters, dressed in livery and carrying a pair of big riding boots, with spurs. He puts them down on the floor where we can see them.*

*happened tonight
before*

JEAN. Miss Julie's gone mad again tonight, Completely mad!
CHRISTINE. Oh, you're here at last?
JEAN. I went with his lordship to the station, and on the way back I just popped into the barn to watch the dancing, and who do I see but Miss Julie leading the dance with the game-keeper? But as soon as she sees me, she rushes across and offers her arm for the ladies' waltz. And then she danced like – I've never known the like! She's mad.
CHRISTINE. She always has been. Especially this last fortnight, since the engagement got broken off.
JEAN. Yes, what about that? He was a gentleman, even if he

wasn't rich. Ach, they don't know their own minds. (*He sits down at the end of the table.*) It's odd, though, that a young lady should choose to stay at home with the servants, on Midsummer Eve, eh? rather than go off to her relations with her father.

CHRISTINE. Oh, I expect she doesn't feel like seeing anyone after that hullaballoo she had with her young man.

JEAN. Very likely! He knew how to stand up for himself, though. Know how it happened, Christine? I saw it, you know, though I took care not to let on I had.

CHRISTINE. No! You saw it?

JEAN. Indeed I did. They were down at the stable yard one evening, and Miss Julie was putting him through his paces, as she called it – do you know what that meant? She made him leap over her riding whip, the way you teach a dog to jump. He leaped twice, and each time she gave him a cut; but the third time, he snatched the whip out of her hand and broke it across his knee. And that was the last we saw of him.

CHRISTINE. Was that what happened? You can't mean it.

JEAN. Yes, that's the way it was. Now, what have you got to tempt me with this evening, Christine?

CHRISTINE (*serves from the pan and lays a place*). Oh, just a bit of kidney I cut from the joint.

JEAN (*smells the food*). Lovely! *Ceci est mon grand délice!* (*He feels the plate.*) You might have warmed the plate, though.

CHRISTINE. You're fussier than his lordship himself, once you start. (*She pulls his hair affectionately.*)

JEAN. (*angrily*). Don't pull my hair. You know how sensitive I am.

CHRISTINE. Now, now. It's only love.

JEAN *eats.* CHRISTINE *brings a bottle of beer.*

JEAN. Beer – on midsummer eve? No, thank you. I can do better than that. (*He opens a drawer in the table and takes out a bottle of red wine with yellow sealing-wax on the cork.*) See that? Yellow seal! Give me a glass, now. A wine glass, I'm drinking this *pur.*

CHRISTINE (*goes back to the stove and puts a small saucepan on*). God have mercy on whoever gets you for a husband. I never met such a fusspot.

JEAN. Oh, rubbish. You'd be jolly pleased to get a gentleman like me. And I don't think you've lost anything through people calling you my fiancée. (*He tastes the wine.*) Good! Very good! Just not quite sufficently *chambré*. (*He warms the glass with his hand.*) We bought this one in Dijon. Four francs a litre it cost – and then there was the bottling – and the duty. What are you cooking now? The smell's infernal.

CHRISTINE. Oh, some filthy muck Miss Julie wants for Diana.

JEAN. Please express yourself more delicately, Christine. But why should you have to cook for that confounded dog on midsummer eve? Is it ill?

CHRISTINE. It's ill all right! It managed to slip out with the gatekeeper's pug, and now it's in trouble – and *that* Miss Julie won't allow.

JEAN. Miss Julie is stuck-up about some things, in others she demeans herself, exactly like her ladyship when she was alive. She was most at home in the kitchen or the stables, but one horse wasn't enough to pull her carriage. She went around with dirty cuffs, but there had to be a crest on every button. Miss Julie, now, to return to her – she doesn't bother about herself and her person. To my mind, she is not what one would call a lady. Just now, when she was dancing in the barn, she grabbed the gamekeeper from Anna and made him dance with her. We'd never do that – but that's how it is when the gentry try to act common – they become really common. But she's a magnificent creature! What a figure! Ah! What shoulders! and – etcetera!

CHRISTINE. No need to overdo it. I've heard what Clara says, and she dresses her.

JEAN. Oh, Clara! You women are always jealous of each other. I've been out riding with her – and the way she dances – !

CHRISTINE. Well, aren't you going to dance with me, when I'm ready?

JEAN. Yes, of course.

CHRISTINE. Promise?

JEAN. Promise? When I say I'll do a thing, I do it. Thank you for that, it was very nice. (*He corks the bottle.*)

MISS JULIE (*in the doorway, talking to someone outside*). I'll be back immediately. Don't wait for me.

JEAN *hides the bottle in the drawer of the table and gets up respectfully.*

MISS JULIE (*enters and goes up to* CHRISTINE *by the stove*). Well, is it ready?

CHRISTINE *indicates that* JEAN *is present.*

JEAN (*gallantly*). Have you ladies secrets to discuss?

MISS JULIE (*flips him in the face with her handkerchief*). Don't be inquisitive!

JEAN. Ah! Charming, that smell of violets.

MISS JULIE (*coquettishly*). Impertinent! So you know about perfumes, too? You certainly know how to dance – stop looking, now, go away!

JEAN (*boldly, yet respectfully*). Is this some magic brew you ladies are preparing on midsummer eve, which will reveal the future and show whom fate has in store for you?

MISS JULIE (*sharply*). You'd need sharp eyes to see him. (*To* CHRISTINE.) Pour it into a bottle, and cork it well. Come now, and dance a schottische with me, Jean.

JEAN (*slowly*). I don't wish to seem disrespectful, but this dance I had promised to Christine –

MISS JULIE. Well, she can have another dance with you, can't you, Christine? Won't you lend me Jean?

CHRISTINE. That's hardly up to me. If Miss Julie condescends, it's not his place to refuse. Go ahead, Jean, and thank madam for the honour.

JEAN. To be frank, without wishing to offend, I wonder if it would be wise for Miss Julie to dance twice in succession with the same partner. These people soon start talking –

MISS JULIE (*flares up*). Talking? What kind of talk? What do you mean?

JEAN (*politely*). If madam doesn't understand, I must speak more plainly. It looks bad if you show a preference for one

110

of your servants while others are waiting to be similarly honoured –

MISS JULIE. Preference! What an idea! I am astounded. I, the lady of the house, honour my servants by attending their dance, and when I take the floor I want to dance with someone who knows how to lead. I don't want to be made ridiculous –

JEAN. As madam commands. I am at your service.

MISS JULIE (*softly*). Don't regard it as a command. Tonight we are ordinary people trying to be happy, and all rank is laid aside. Come, give me your arm! Don't worry, Christine! I won't steal your lover!

JEAN *offers* MISS JULIE *his arm, and escorts her out.*

PANTOMIME

This should be played as though the actress were actually alone. When the occasion calls for it she should turn her back on the audience. She does not look towards them; and must not hasten her movements as though afraid lest they should grow impatient.

CHRISTINE *alone. A violin can be faintly heard in the distance, playing a schottische.* CHRISTINE *hums in time with the music; clears up after* JEAN, *washes the plate at the sink, dries it and puts it away in a cupboard. Then she removes her apron, takes a small mirror from a drawer, props it against the pot of lilac on the table; lights a candle and warms a curling-iron, with which she then crisps the hair over her forehead. Goes out into the doorway and listens. Returns to the table. Finds* MISS JULIE'S *handkerchief, which the latter has forgotten; picks it up and smells it; then, spreads it out, as though thinking of something else, stretches it, smooths it, folds it into quarters, etc.*

JEAN (*enters alone*). No, she really *is* mad! What a way to dance! Everyone was grinning at her from behind the doors. What do you make of it, Christine?

CHRISTINE. Oh, she's got her monthly coming on, and then

she always acts strange. Well, are you going to dance with me now?

JEAN. You're not angry with me for leaving you like that – ?

CHRISTINE. No, a little thing like that doesn't bother me. Besides, I know my place –

JEAN (*puts his arm round her waist*). You're a sensible girl, Christine. You'd make a good wife –

MISS JULIE (*enters; is disagreeably surprised; speaks with forced lightness*). Well, you're a fine gentleman, running away from your partner like that!

JEAN. On the contrary, Miss Julie. As you see, I have hastened to return to the partner I forsook!

MISS JULIE (*changes her tone*). Do you know, you dance magnificently. But why are you wearing uniform on midsummer eve? Take it off at once.

JEAN. Then I must ask your ladyship to step outside for a moment. I have my black coat here – (*Gestures right.*)

MISS JULIE. Does my presence embarrass you? Can't you change a coat with me here? You'd better go into your room, then. Or stay, and I'll turn my back.

JEAN. With your ladyship's permission.

He goes right. We see his arm as he changes his coat.

MISS JULIE (*to* CHRISTINE). Christine, Jean is very familiar with you. Are you engaged to him?

CHRISTINE. Engaged? If you like. We call it that.

MISS JULIE. Call – ?

CHRISTINE. Well, you've been engaged yourself, madam –

MISS JULIE. We were properly engaged.

CHRISTINE. Didn't come to anything, though, did it?

JEAN *enters in black tails and a black bowler hat.*

MISS JULIE. *Très gentil, monsieur Jean! Très gentil!*

JEAN. *Vous voulez plaisanter, madame!*

MISS JULIE. *Et vous voulez parler français!* Where did you learn that?

JEAN. In Switzerland. I was wine waiter at the biggest hotel in Lucerne.

ad a bit to drink

MISS JULIE. You look quite the gentleman in those tails. *Charmant!* (*She sits at the table.*)

JEAN. Oh, you're flattering me.

MISS JULIE (*haughtily*). Flattering *you*?

JEAN. My natural modesty forbids me to suppose that you would pay a truthful compliment to one so humble as myself, so I assumed you were exaggerating, for which I believe the polite word is flattering.

MISS JULIE. Where did you learn to talk like that? You must have spent a lot of your time at the theatre.

JEAN. Yes. And I've been around a bit, too.

MISS JULIE. But you were born here, weren't you?

JEAN. My father worked on the next farm to yours. I used to see you when I was a child, though you wouldn't remember me.

MISS JULIE. No, really?

JEAN. Yes. I remember one time especially – no, I oughtn't to mention that.

MISS JULIE. Oh yes! Tell me. Come on! Just this once.

JEAN. No, I really couldn't now. Some other time, perhaps.

MISS JULIE. Some other time means never. Is it so dangerous to tell it now?

JEAN. It isn't dangerous, but I'd rather not. Look at her! (*He indicates* CHRISTINE, *who has fallen asleep in a chair by the stove.*)

MISS JULIE. A charming wife she'll make. Does she snore too?

JEAN. She doesn't do that, but she talks in her sleep.

MISS JULIE (*cynically*). How do you know?

JEAN. (*coolly*). I've heard her.

Pause. They look at each other.

MISS JULIE. Why don't you sit?

JEAN. I wouldn't permit myself to do that in your presence.

MISS JULIE. But if I order you to?

JEAN. Then I shall obey.

MISS JULIE. Sit, then. No, wait. Can you give me something to drink first?

JEAN. I don't know what we have in the ice-cabinet. Only beer, I think.

MISS JULIE. What do you mean, only beer? My taste is very simple. I prefer it to wine.

JEAN *takes a bottle of beer from the ice-cabinet, opens it, gets a glass and plate from the cupboard and serves her.*

JEAN. Mademoiselle!

MISS JULIE. Thank you. Won't you have something yourself?

JEAN. I'm not much of a beer drinker, but if madam orders me –

MISS JULIE. Orders? Surely you know that a gentleman should never allow a lady to drink alone.

JEAN. That's perfectly true. (*He opens another bottle and pours a glass.*)

MISS JULIE. Drink my health, now! (JEAN *hesitates.*) Are you shy?

JEAN (*kneels in a parody of a romantic attitude, and raises his glass*). To my mistress's health!

MISS JULIE. Bravo! Now kiss my shoe, and the ceremony is complete.

JEAN *hesitates, then boldly takes her foot in his hands and kisses it lightly.*

MISS JULIE. Excellent. You ought to have been an actor.

JEAN (*gets up*). We mustn't go on like this, Miss Julie. Someone might come in and see us.

MISS JULIE. What then?

JEAN. People would talk, that's all. And if you knew how their tongues were wagging up there just now –

MISS JULIE. What kind of thing were they saying? Tell me. Sit down.

JEAN (*sits*). I don't want to hurt you, but they were using expressions which – which hinted that – well, you can guess! You aren't a child, and when people see a lady drinking alone with a man – let alone a servant – on Midsummer Eve – then –

MISS JULIE. Then what? Anyway, we're not alone. Christine is here.

JEAN. Asleep.

MISS JULIE. Then I shall wake her. (*She gets up.*) Christine! Christine! Are you asleep?

CHRISTINE *mumbles to herself in her sleep.*

MISS JULIE. Christine! My God, she is asleep!

CHRISTINE (*in her sleep*). Are his lordship's boots brushed? Put on the coffee. Quickly, quickly, quickly! (*She laughs, then grunts.*)

MISS JULIE (*takes her by the nose*). Will you wake up?

JEAN (*sharply*). Leave her alone!

MISS JULIE (*haughtily*). What!

JEAN. People who stand at a stove all day get tired when night comes. And sleep is something to be respected –

MISS JULIE (*changes tack*). A gallant thought, and one that does you honour. (*She holds out her hand to* JEAN.) Come outside then, and pick some lilac for me.

During the following dialogue, CHRISTINE *wakes and wanders drowsily right to go to bed.*

JEAN. With you?

MISS JULIE. With me.

JEAN. Impossible. I couldn't.

MISS JULIE. I don't understand. Surely you don't imagine – ?

JEAN. I don't, but other people might.

MISS JULIE. What? That I should have an *amour* with a servant?

JEAN. I'm not being conceited, but such things have happened – and to these people, nothing is sacred.

MISS JULIE. Quite the little aristocrat, aren't you? *important quote*

JEAN. Yes, I am.

MISS JULIE. If I choose to step down –

JEAN. Don't step down, Miss Julie, take my advice. No one will believe you did it freely. People will always say you fell –

MISS JULIE. I have a higher opinion of people than you. Come and see! Come.

She fixes him with her eyes.

JEAN. You know, you're strange.

1. Jean has told Julie what to do – not the sort of thing he should do

MISS JULIE. Perhaps. But so are you. Everything is strange. Life, people, everything, is a scum which drifts, drifts on and on across the water until it sinks, sinks. I have a dream which recurs from time to time, and I'm reminded of it now. I've climbed to the top of a pillar, and am sitting there, and I can see no way to descend. When I look down, I become dizzy, but I must come down – but I haven't the courage to jump. I can't stay up there, and I long to fall, but I don't fall. And yet I know I shall find no peace till I come down, no rest till I come down, down to the ground. And if I could get down, I should want to burrow my way deep into the earth. . . . Have you ever felt anything like that?

JEAN. No. I dream that I'm lying under a high tree in a dark wood. I want to climb, up, up to the top, and look round over the bright landscape where the sun is shining – plunder the bird's nest up there where the gold eggs lie. And I climb and climb, but the trunk is so thick and slippery, and it's so far to the first branch. But I know that if I could only get to that first branch, I'd climb my way to the top as though up a ladder. I haven't reached it yet, but I shall reach it, even if it's only in a dream.

MISS JULIE. Why do we stand here talking about dreams? Come, now! Just into the park!

She offers him her arm, and they go.

JEAN. We must sleep with nine midsummer flowers under our pillows tonight, Miss Julie, and our dreams will come true!

They turn in the doorway. JEAN *puts a hand to one of his eyes.*

MISS JULIE. Have you something in your eye?

JEAN. It's nothing. Only a speck of dust. It'll be all right soon.

MISS JULIE. My sleeve must have brushed it. Sit down and I'll take it out. (*She takes him by the arm, makes him sit, takes his head and pushes it backwards, and tries to remove the dust with the corner of her handkerchief.*) Sit still now, quite still! (*She slaps his hands.*) Come, obey me! I believe you're trembling, you great, strong lout! (*She feels his bicep.*) What muscles you have!

116

JEAN (*warningly*). Miss Julie!

MISS JULIE. Yes, monsieur Jean?

JEAN. *Attention! Je ne suis qu'un homme!*

MISS JULIE. Sit still, will you! There! Now it's gone. Kiss my
hand and thank me.

JEAN (*gets up*). Miss Julie, listen to me. Christine's gone to bed
now – will you listen to me!

MISS JULIE. Kiss my hand first.

JEAN. Listen to me!

MISS JULIE. Kiss my hand first.

JEAN. All right. But you've only yourself to blame.

MISS JULIE. For what?

JEAN. For what? Are you a child? You're twenty-five. Don't
you know it's dangerous to play with fire?

MISS JULIE. Not for me. I am insured.

JEAN (*boldly*). No, you're not. And if you are, there's inflam-
mable material around that isn't.

MISS JULIE. Meaning you?

JEAN. Yes. Not because I'm me, but because I'm a young
man –

MISS JULIE. Of handsome appearance! What incredible con-
ceit! A Don Juan, perhaps? Or a Joseph! Yes, upon my
word, I do believe you're a Joseph!

JEAN. Do you?

MISS JULIE. I almost fear it.

JEAN *moves boldly forward and tries to take her round the waist
to kiss her.*

MISS JULIE (*slaps him*). Stop it!

JEAN. Are you joking or serious?

MISS JULIE. Serious.

JEAN. Then you were being serious just now too. You play
games too seriously, and that's dangerous. Well, now I'm
tired of this game and with your permission I'll get back to
my work. His lordship's boots must be ready in time, and it's
long past midnight.

MISS JULIE. Forget the boots.

JEAN. No. They're part of my job, which doesn't include being your playmate. And never will. I flatter myself I'm above that.

MISS JULIE. Aren't we proud!

JEAN. In some respects. In others, not.

MISS JULIE. Have you ever been in love?

JEAN. We don't use that word. But I've been fond of a lot of girls, and once I was sick because I couldn't get the one I wanted. Yes, sick, do you hear, like those princes in the Arabian Nights, who couldn't eat or sleep because of love.

MISS JULIE. Who was she? (JEAN *is silent.*) Who was she?

JEAN. You cannot order me to answer that.

MISS JULIE. If I ask you as an equal? As a friend! Who was she?

JEAN. You.

MISS JULIE (*sits*). How absurd!

JEAN. Yes, if you like. It was absurd. Look, this was the story I didn't want to tell you just now – but now I will tell you. Do you know how the world looks from down there? No, you don't. Like hawks and eagles, whose backs one seldom sees because most of the time they hover above you! I lived in a hut with seven brothers and sisters and a pig, out in the grey fields where never a tree grew. But from the window I could see the wall of his lordship's park, with apple trees rising above it. It was the Garden of Paradise, and there stood many evil angels with flaming swords to guard it. But despite them I and other boys found a way in to the tree of life – You despise me now?

MISS JULIE. Oh, I suppose all boys steal apples.

JEAN. You can say that now, but you do despise me. However. One day I entered the garden with my mother, to weed the onion beds. On one side of the garden stood a Turkish pavilion in the shadow of jasmine trees and overgrown with honeysuckle. I'd never seen such a building. I wondered what it could be for. People went in and came out again; and, one day, the door was left open. I crept in and saw the walls hung with pictures of kings and emperors, and there were red velvet curtains on the windows with tassels – ah, now you understand! It was the lavatory. I – (*He breaks a*

MISS JULIE. I know these people, and I love them, as I know they love me. Let them come here, and I'll prove it to you.

JEAN. No, Miss Julie, they don't love you. They take your food, but once you've turned your back they spit at you. Believe me! Listen to them, listen to what they're singing! No, don't listen!

MISS JULIE (listens). What are they singing?

JEAN. It's a filthy song. About you and me.

MISS JULIE. How dare they! The traitors – !

JEAN. Yes, but that's what they're like. One can't fight them. One can only run away.

MISS JULIE. Run away? But where? We can't go out – or into Christine's room!

JEAN. No. Into my room, then. We can't bother about conventions now. And you can trust me. I am your true, loyal and respectful – friend.

MISS JULIE. But suppose – suppose they look for you in there?

JEAN. I'll bolt the door. And if anyone tries to break in, I'll shoot. Come! (He drops to his knees.) Please! Come!

MISS JULIE (urgently). You promise –

JEAN. I swear.

MISS JULIE runs out right. JEAN hastens after her.

BALLET

peasants stream in, wearing their best clothes, with flowers in hats and a fiddler at their head. A barrel of beer and a keg snapps decorated with greenery are set on a table, glasses are ced, and they drink. They form a ring and dance and mime, : 'One young girl in a big dark wood!' When this is finished, o out singing.

JULIE *enters, alone. She sees the chaos in the kitchen, er hands, then takes out a powder puff and powders her*

nters, agitated). There – you see! And you heard. Do ink you can possibly stay here now?

LIE. No, I don't. But what can we do?

flower from the lilac and holds it beneath MISS JULIE'S *nose.)* I'd never been inside the palace, never seen anything except the church – but this was more beautiful – and however my thoughts might stray, they always returned there. And gradually I began to long just once to experience the full ecstasy of actually – *enfin*, I tip-toed inside, saw and marvelled. But then – someone's coming! There was only one exit – for the lords and ladies, But for me – there was another – and I had no choice but to take it. (MISS JULIE, *who has taken the lilac blossom, lets it fall on the table.)* Then I ran, broke through a raspberry hedge, charged across a strawberry patch, and found myself on a terrace with a rose garden. There I saw a pink dress and a pair of white stockings. You. I hid under a pile of weeds – *under*, can you imagine that? under thistles that pricked me and wet earth that stank like me. And I looked at you as you walked among the roses, and I thought: 'If it is true that a thief can enter heaven and dwell with the angels, then it's strange that a peasant's child here on earth cannot enter the great park and play with the Count's daughter.'

MISS JULIE (romantically). Do you suppose all poor children have had the same ideas as you?

JEAN (at first hesitant, then with conviction). Have *all* poor – ? Yes! Of course! Of course!

MISS JULIE. It must be a terrible misfortune to be poor.

JEAN (deeply cut, speaks with strong emotion). Oh, Miss Julie! Oh! A dog may lie on the Countess's sofa, a horse may have its nose patted by a young lady's hand, but a servant – ! (*He changes his tone.*) Oh, now and then a man has strength enough to hoist himself up in the world, but how often does it happen? But do you know what I did? I ran down into the millstream with my clothes on. They dragged me out and beat me. But the following Sunday, when my father and all the others had gone to visit my grandmother, I managed to fix things so that I stayed at home. And then I scrubbed myself with soap and hot water, put on my best clothes, and went to church, in order that I might see you. I saw you, and returned home, determined to die. But I wanted to die beautifully, and pleasantly, without pain. Then I remembered it was dangerous to sleep under an elder bush. We had a big one, in flower. I stripped it of everything it held, and then I lay down in the oat-bin. Have you ever noticed how beautiful oats are? Soft to the touch like human skin. Well, I shut the lid and closed my eyes. I fell asleep, and woke up feeling really very ill. But I didn't die, as you can see. What did I want? I don't know. I had no hope of winning you, of course – but you were a symbol to me of the hopelessness of my ever climbing out of the class in which I was born.

MISS JULIE. Do you know you're quite a *raconteur*? Did you ever go to school?

JEAN. A bit. But I've read a lot of novels, and gone to theatres. And I've heard gentry talk. That's where I've learned most.

MISS JULIE. Do you listen to what we say?

JEAN. Certainly! And I've heard plenty, too, sitting on the coachman's box or rowing the boat. One time I heard you and a lady friend –

MISS JULIE. Indeed? What did you hear?

JEAN. Oh, I wouldn't care to repeat it. But it surprised me a little. I couldn't imagine where you'd learned all those words. Maybe at bottom there isn't as big a difference as people suppose between people and – people.

MISS JULIE. Oh, nonsense. We don't act like you do when we're engaged.

JEAN (*looks at her*). Are you sure? Come, Miss Julie, you don't have to play the innocent with me –

MISS JULIE. The man to whom I offered my love was a bastard.

JEAN. That's what they always say – afterwards.

MISS JULIE. Always?

JEAN. I've heard the expression several times before on similar occasions.

MISS JULIE. What occasions?

JEAN. Like the one in question. The last time I actually slept with a lady –

MISS JULIE (*rises*). Be quiet! I don't wish to hear any more.

JEAN. *She* didn't want to, either. Strange. Well, have permission to go to bed?

MISS JULIE (*softly*). Go to bed? On midsummer eve

JEAN. Yes. Dancing with that pack up there doesn' amuse me.

MISS JULIE. Get the key of the boat and row me o lake. I want to see the sun rise.

JEAN. Is that wise?

MISS JULIE. You speak as though you were frighten reputation.

JEAN. Why not? I don't want to make myself a laug and maybe get sacked without a reference, no beginning to make my way. And I think I ha responsibility towards Christine.

MISS JULIE. Oh, I see, it's Christine now –

JEAN. Yes, but you too. Take my advice. Go back and go to bed.

MISS JULIE. Am *I* to obey *you*?

JEAN. For once. For your own sake, I beg y drowsiness makes one drunk, one's head grow bed. Besides – if my ears don't deceive me – vants are coming here to look for me. And together, you are lost!

Approaching voices are heard, singing.

VOICES. One young girl in a big dark wood!
Tridiridi-ralla, tridiridi-ra!
Met a boy she never should!
Tridiridi-ralla-ra!

Oh, lay me on the grass so soft!
Tridiridi-ralla, tridiridi-ra!
So her mm-mm-mm she lost!
Tridiridi-ralla-ra!

Oh, thank you dear, but I mu
Tridiridi-ralla, tridiridi-ra!
Another loves me now ... o
Tridiridi-ralla-ra!

JEAN. Go away – travel – far away from here –

MISS JULIE. Travel? Yes, but where?

JEAN. To Switzerland, to the Italian lakes! Have you never been there?

MISS JULIE. No. Is it beautiful there?

JEAN. Ah! An eternal summer! Oranges, laurel trees – ah!

MISS JULIE. But what shall we do there?

JEAN. I'll start a hotel. *De luxe* – for *de luxe* people.

MISS JULIE. Hotel?

JEAN. Ah, that's a life, believe me! New faces all the time, new languages! Never a minute for worry or nerves, or wondering what to do. There's work to be done every minute, bells ringing night and day, trains whistling, carriages coming and going, and all the time the golden sovereigns roll into the till. Yes, that's the life!

MISS JULIE. It sounds exciting. But – I – ?

JEAN. Shall be the mistress of the house; the pearl of the establishment. With your looks – and your style – why, we're made! It'll be terrific! You'll sit at your desk like a queen, setting your slaves in motion by pressing an electric bell. The guests will file before your throne, humbly laying their tribute upon your table – you've no idea how people tremble when they get a bill in their hand. I shall salt the bills, and you shall sugar them with your prettiest smile! Oh, let's get away from here! (*He takes a timetable from his pocket.*) Now, at once, by the next train! We'll be in Malmö by 6.30, Hamburg 8.40 tomorrow morning, Frankfurt to Basel will take a day, through the Gothard Pass – we'll be in Como in, let me see, three days. Three days!

MISS JULIE. It sounds wonderful. But, Jean – you must give me courage. Tell me you love me. Come and kiss me.

JEAN (*hesitates*). I'd like to – but I daren't. Not in this house – not again. Of course I love you – can you doubt it, Miss Julie?

MISS JULIE (*shy, feminine*). *Miss!* Call me Julie! There are no barriers between us now. Call me Julie!

JEAN (*tormented*). I can't! There are still barriers between us – there always will be, as long as we're in this house. There's the past, there's his lordship – I've never met anyone I respected as I do him – I only have to see his gloves on a chair and I feel like a small boy – I only have to hear that bell ring and I jump like a frightened horse – and when I see his boots standing there, so straight and proud, I cringe. (*He kicks the boots.*) Superstition – ideas shoved into our heads when we're children – but we can escape them. Come to another country, a republic, and others will cringe before my porter's livery – yes, they'll cringe, I tell you, but I shan't! I wasn't born to cringe – I'm a man, I've got character, just let me get my fingers on that first branch and watch me climb! Today I'm a servant, but next year I'll own my own hotel, in ten years I'll be a landed gentleman! Then I'll go to Rumania, get a decoration – why, I might – might, mind you – end up with a title.

MISS JULIE. How wonderful!

JEAN. Oh, in Rumania I could buy myself a title. I'd be a Count, and you'd be a Countess. My Countess!

MISS JULIE. What do I care about all that? That's what I'm giving up now. Tell me you love me, otherwise – yes, otherwise – what am I?

JEAN. I'll tell you a thousand times – later. Only – not here. Above all, no emotional scenes, or it'll be all up with us. We must think this over coolly, like sensible people. (*He takes a cigar, cuts and lights it.*) Sit down there now, and I'll sit here and we'll talk as though nothing had happened.

MISS JULIE (*desperately*). Oh, my God! Have you no feelings?

JEAN. I? No one has more feelings than I. But I can control them.

MISS JULIE. A moment ago you could kiss my shoe – and now – !

JEAN (*harshly*). That was a moment ago. Now we've something else to think about.

MISS JULIE. Don't speak so harshly to me.

JEAN. I'm not speaking harshly. I'm talking sense. One folly has been committed, don't let's commit any more. His lordship may be here any moment, and by then we've got to decide what we're going to do with our lives. What do you think of my plans for our future? Do you approve of them?

MISS JULIE. They seem to me quite sensible but – just one question. A big project like that needs a lot of capital. Have you that?

JEAN (*chews his cigar*). I? Certainly. I have my professional expertise, my experience, my knowledge of languages. We've adequate capital, I should say.

MISS JULIE. But all that doesn't add up to the price of a railway ticket.

JEAN. That's perfectly true; which is why I need a backer to advance me the money.

MISS JULIE. Where are you going to find one quickly?

JEAN. You'll find one, if you come with me.

MISS JULIE. I couldn't. And I haven't any money of my own.

Pause.

JEAN. Then our whole plan collapses.

MISS JULIE. And – ?

JEAN. Things must stay as they are.

MISS JULIE. Do you suppose I'm going to remain under this roof as your whore? With *them* sniggering at me behind their fingers? Do you think I can look my father in the face after this? No! Take me away from here, from the shame and the dishonour – oh, what have I done, my God, my God! (*Sobs*)

JEAN. Come, don't start that. What have you done? The same as many others before you.

MISS JULIE (*screams convulsively*). Oh, now you despise me! I'm falling – I'm falling – !

JEAN. Fall down to me, and I'll lift you up again

MISS JULIE. What dreadful power drew me to you? The attraction of the weak to the strong? Of the faller to the climber? Or was it love? Was this love? Do you know what love is?

JEAN. I? Yes, of course. Do you think I've never had a woman before?

MISS JULIE. How can you think and talk like that?

JEAN. That's life as I've learned it. And that's me. Now calm down and stop acting the lady. We're both in the same boat now. Come here, my girl, and I'll give you a glass of wine. (*He opens drawer, takes out the bottle of wine and fills two used glasses.*)

MISS JULIE. Where did you get that wine from?

JEAN. The cellar.

MISS JULIE. My father's burgundy!

JEAN. Is it too good for his son-in-law?

MISS JULIE. And I drink beer! I!

JEAN. That only proves you have an inferior palate to mine.

MISS JULIE. Thief!

JEAN. Going to tell?

MISS JULIE. Oh, oh! Accomplice to a sneakthief! Was I drunk, was I dreaming? Midsummer night! The night of innocent happiness –

JEAN. Innocent? Hm!

MISS JULIE (*paces to and fro*). Is there anyone on this earth as miserable as I?

JEAN. Why should you be miserable after such a conquest? Think of Christine in there. Don't you suppose she has feelings too?

MISS JULIE. I thought so just now, but I don't any longer. Servants are servants –

JEAN. And whores are whores.

MISS JULIE (*kneels and clasps her hands*). Oh, God in Heaven, end my miserable life! Save me from this mire into which I'm sinking! Save me, save me!

JEAN. I can't deny I feel sorry for you. When I lay in the onion bed and saw you in the rose garden – I might as well tell you now – I had the same dirty thoughts as any small boy.

MISS JULIE. You – who wanted to die for me?

JEAN. The oat-bin? Oh, that was just talk.

MISS JULIE. A lie?

JEAN (*begins to get sleepy*). More or less. I once read a story in a paper about a sweep who curled up in a wood-chest with some lilacs because he'd had a paternity order brought against him –

MISS JULIE. I see. You're the kind who –

JEAN. Well, I had to think up something. Women always fall for pretty stories.

MISS JULIE. Swine!

JEAN. *Merde!*

MISS JULIE. And now you've managed to see the eagle's back –

JEAN. Not exactly its back.

MISS JULIE. And I was to be the first branch –

JEAN. But the branch was rotten –

MISS JULIE. I was to be the signboard of the hotel –

JEAN. And I the hotel –

MISS JULIE. I was to sit at your desk, attract your customers, fiddle your bills –

JEAN. No, I'd have done that –

MISS JULIE. Can a human soul become so foul?

JEAN. Wash it, then!

MISS JULIE. Servant, lackey, stand up when I speak!

JEAN. Servant's whore, lackey's bitch, shut your mouth and get out of here. You dare to stand there and call me foul? Not one of my class ever behaved the way you've done tonight. Do you think any kitchen-maid would accost a man like you did? Have you ever seen any girl of my class offer her body like that? I've only seen it among animals and prostitutes.

MISS JULIE (*crushed*). You're right. Hit me, trample on me, I've deserved nothing better. I'm worthless – but help me, help me out of this – if there is a way out.

JEAN (*more gently*). I don't want to disclaim my share in the honour of having seduced you, but do you imagine a man in my position would have dared to so much as glance at you if you hadn't invited him? I'm still dumbfounded –

MISS JULIE. And proud.

JEAN. Why not? Though I must confess I found the conquest a little too easy to be really exciting.

MISS JULIE. Hurt me more.

JEAN (*gets up*). No. Forgive me for what I've said. I don't hit defenceless people, least of all women. I can't deny it gratifies me to have found that it was only a gilt veneer that dazzled our humble eyes, that the eagle's back was as scabbed as our own, that the whiteness of those cheeks was only powder, that those polished fingernails had black edges, that that handkerchief was dirty though it smelt of perfume – But on the other hand, it hurts me to have discovered that what I was aspiring towards was not something worthier and more solid. It hurts me to see you sunk so low, to find that deep down you are a kitchen slut. It hurts me, like seeing the autumn flowers whipped to tatters by the rain and trodden into the mud.

MISS JULIE. You speak as though you were already above me.

JEAN. I am. You see, I could make you into a Countess, but you could never make me into a Count.

MISS JULIE. But I am of noble blood, and you can never be that.

JEAN. That's true. But my children could be noblemen, if –

MISS JULIE. But you're a thief. That's something I am not.

JEAN. There are worse things than being a thief. Besides, when I work in a house I regard myself more a less as a member of the family, a child of the house, and people don't call it stealing when a child takes a berry from a bush heavy with fruit. (*His passion rises again.*) Miss Julie, you're a fine woman, much too good for someone like me. You've been the victim of a drunken folly, and you want to cover it up by pretending to yourself that you love me. You don't, unless perhaps physically – and then your love is no better than mine – but I can never be content with being just your animal, and I can never make you love me.

MISS JULIE. Are you sure of that?

JEAN. You mean it might happen? Yes, I could love you easily – you're beautiful, you're refined – (*He approaches her and takes her hand.*) Educated, lovable when you want to be, and once you have awoken a man's passion, it could never die. (*He puts his arm round her waist.*) You are like hot wine, strongly spiced, and a kiss from you – ! (*He tries to lead her out but she slowly tears herself free.*)

MISS JULIE. Let me go! You won't win me like that!

JEAN. How, then? Not like that. Not by caresses and fine

words. Not by thinking of your future, rescuing you from what you've done. How, then?

MISS JULIE. How? How? I don't know. There is no way. I detest you as I detest rats, but I cannot run away from you.

JEAN. Run away with me!

MISS JULIE (*straightens herself*). Run away? Yes, we must run away. But I'm so tired. Give me a glass of wine. I'm so tired. (JEAN *pours her some. She looks at her watch.*) But we must talk first. We have a little time. (*She drains the glass and holds it out for more.*)

JEAN. Don't drink so much, you'll get drunk.

MISS JULIE. What does that matter?

JEAN. What does it matter? It's stupid to get drunk. What were you going to say to me just now?

MISS JULIE. We must run away! But first we must talk – that is, I must talk – so far you've been doing all the talking. You've told me about your life, now I must tell you about myself, so that we know all about each other before we go away together.

JEAN. One moment. Forgive me, but – consider – you may later regret having revealed your private secrets to me.

MISS JULIE. Aren't you my friend?

JEAN. Yes – sometimes. But don't rely on me.

MISS JULIE. You're only saying that. Anyway, everyone else knows. You see, my mother was a commoner, of quite humble birth. She was brought up with ideas about equality, freedom for women and all that. And she had a decided aversion to marriage. So when my father proposed to her, she replied that she would never become his wife, but that he could become her lover. My father told her that he had no desire to see the woman he loved enjoy less respect than himself. When she explained that the world's respect did not concern her, he agreed to her conditions. But now he was cut off from his social circle and confined to his domestic life, which could not satisfy him. And then? I came into the world, against my mother's wish as far as I can gather. She wanted to bring me up as a child of nature, and into the bargain I was to learn everything that a boy has to learn, so that I might stand as an example of how a woman can be as good as a man. I had to wear boy's clothes, and learn to look after horses – though I was never allowed to enter the cowshed. I had to groom and saddle them, and hunt – even learn to slaughter animals. That was horrible. Meanwhile, on the estate, all the men were set to perform the women's tasks, and the women the men's – so that it began to fail, and we became the laughing-stock of the district. In the end my father put his foot down, and everything was changed back to the way he wanted it. That was when they married. Then my mother fell ill – what illness, I don't know – but she often had convulsions, hid herself, in the attic and the garden, and sometimes stayed out all night. Then there was the great fire which you have heard about. The house, the stables and the cowshed were all burned down, under circumstances suggesting arson – for the accident happened the very day our quarterly insurance had expired, and the premium my father sent had been delayed through the inefficiency of the servant carrying it, so that it hadn't arrived in time. (*She fills her glass and drinks.*)

JEAN. Don't drink so much.

MISS JULIE. Oh, what does it matter? So we were left penniless, and had to sleep in the carriages. My father couldn't think where he would be able to find the money to rebuild the house, as he'd cut himself off from his old friends. Then mother advised him to ask for a loan from an old friend of hers, a brick merchant who lived in the neighbourhood. Father got the money, free of interest, which rather surprised him. So the house was rebuilt. (*She drinks again.*) Do you know who burned the house down?

JEAN. Your mother!

MISS JULIE. Do you know who the brick merchant was?

JEAN. Your mother's lover!

MISS JULIE. Do you know whose the money was?

JEAN. Wait a moment. No, that I don't know.

MISS JULIE. It was my mother's.

JEAN. His lordship's too, then. Unless he'd made a marriage settlement.

MISS JULIE. No, there wasn't any marriage settlement. My mother had had a little money of her own, which she didn't want my father to have control of. So she entrusted it to her – friend.

JEAN. Who kept it!

MISS JULIE. Exactly. He kept it. All this came to my father's knowledge – but he couldn't start an action, repay his wife's lover, or prove that the money was his wife's. It was my mother's revenge on him, for taking control of the house out of her hands. He was on the verge of shooting himself – the rumour was that he had done so, but had failed to kill himself. Well, he lived; and he made my mother pay for what she had done. Those five years were dreadful for me, I can tell you. I was sorry for my father, but I took my mother's side, because I didn't know the circumstances. I'd learned from her to distrust and hate men – she hated men. And I swore to her that I would never be a slave to any man.

JEAN. But then you got engaged to that young lawyer?

MISS JULIE. So that he should be my slave.

JEAN. And he wasn't willing?

MISS JULIE. He was willing enough, but he didn't get the chance. I tired of him.

JEAN. I saw it. In the stable.

MISS JULIE. Saw what?

JEAN. How he broke off the engagement.

MISS JULIE. That's a lie! It was I who broke it off! Has he been saying he did it, the little liar?

JEAN. He wasn't a liar. You hate men, Miss Julie.

MISS JULIE. Yes. Most of the time. But sometimes – when nature burns – ! Oh, God! Will the fire never die?

JEAN. You hate me too?

MISS JULIE. Immeasurably! I'd like to shoot you like an animal –

JEAN. 'The offender gets two years penal servitude and the animal is shot.' That's the law for bestiality, isn't it? But you've nothing to shoot with. So what shall we do?

MISS JULIE. Go away!

JEAN. To torment each other to death?

MISS JULIE. No. To be happy – for two days – a week – as long as one can be happy – and then – die –

JEAN. Die? Don't be stupid. I'd rather start the hotel than do that.

MISS JULIE (*not hearing him*). – on the Lake of Como, where the sun always shines, where the laurels are green at Christmas, and the orange-trees flame!

JEAN. Actually, it's always raining on the Lake of Como, and I never saw any oranges there except in the grocers' shops. But it's a good spot for tourists, there are a lot of villas to hire out to loving couples, and that's a profitable industry – you know why? Because they lease them for six months, and then leave after three weeks.

MISS JULIE (*naïvely*). Why after three weeks?

JEAN. They quarrel, of course! But they have to pay the full rent, and then you hire it out again. So it goes on, couple after couple. For love must go on, if not for very long.

MISS JULIE. You don't want to die with me?

JEAN. I don't want to die at all. Partly because I like life, and partly because I regard suicide as a crime against the Providence which gave us life.

MISS JULIE. You believe in God – *you*?

JEAN. Certainly I do. And I go to church every other Sunday. Quite frankly now, I'm tired of all this, and I'm going to bed.

MISS JULIE. I see. And you think I'm going to rest content with that? Don't you know what a man owes to a woman he has shamed?

JEAN (*takes out his purse and throws a silver coin on the table*). Here. I always pay my debts.

MISS JULIE (*pretends not to notice the insult*). Do you know what the law says – ?

JEAN. Unfortunately the law doesn't demand any penalty from a woman who seduces a man.

MISS JULIE. Can you see any other solution than that we should go away, marry, and part?

JEAN. And if I refuse to enter into this *mésalliance*?

MISS JULIE. *Mésalliance*?

132

JEAN. Yes – for me! I've got a better heritage than you. None of my ancestors committed arson.

MISS JULIE. How do you know?

JEAN. You couldn't prove it, because we don't have any family records – except with the police. But I've studied your pedigree in a book I found on the table in the drawing room. Do you know who the first of your ancestors to get a title was? He was a miller who let the King sleep with his wife one night during the Danish war. I haven't any noble ancestors like that – I haven't any noble ancestors at all. But I could become one myself.

MISS JULIE. This is my reward for opening my heart to a servant, for giving my family's honour – !

JEAN. Honour? Don't say I didn't tell you. One shouldn't drink, it loosens the tongue. And that's bad.

MISS JULIE. Oh God, how I regret it, how I regret it! If you at least loved me – !

JEAN. For the last time – what do you want? Shall I burst into tears, shall I jump over your riding crop, shall I kiss you, trick you down to Lake Como for three weeks, and then – what? What shall I do? What do you want me to do? This is beginning to get tiresome. It's always like this when one gets involved with women. Miss Julie! I see you are unhappy, I know you are suffering, but I do not understand you! We don't fool around like you do – we don't hate – love is a game we play when we have a little time free from work, but we aren't free all day and all night like you! I think you must be ill. Yes, undoubtedly, you're ill.

MISS JULIE. Speak kindly to me, Jean. Treat me like a human being.

JEAN. Act like one yourself, then. You spit at me, and won't let me wipe it off – on you.

MISS JULIE. Help me, help me! Just tell me what to do. Where shall I go.

JEAN. For God's sake! If I only knew!

MISS JULIE. I've been mad, I know I've been mad, but isn't there some way out?

JEAN. Stay here, and keep calm. No one knows.

MISS JULIE. Impossible. The servants know. And Christine.

JEAN. They don't know for sure. They wouldn't really believe it could happen.

MISS JULIE (*hesitantly*). But – it could happen again.

JEAN. That is true.

MISS JULIE. And – then?

JEAN (*frightened*). Then? My God, why didn't I think of that? Yes, there's only one answer – you must go away. At once. I can't come with you – then we'd be finished – you must go alone – far away – anywhere.

MISS JULIE. Alone? Where? I can't!

JEAN. You must! And before his lordship returns. If you stay, you know what'll happen. Once one has made a mistake one wants to go on, because the damage has already been done. Then one gets more and more careless and – in the end one gets found out. So go! You can write to his lordship later and tell him everything – except that it was me! He'll never guess that. And I don't suppose he'll be over-keen to find out who it was.

MISS JULIE. I'll go, if you'll come with me.

JEAN. Are you mad, woman? Miss Julie run away with her servant! It'd be in the newspapers in a couple of days, and his lordship'd never live that down.

MISS JULIE. I can't go. I can't stay. Help me! I'm so tired, so dreadfully tired. Order me! Make me do something! I can't think, I can't act –

JEAN. Now you see what a contemptible creature you are! Why do you prink yourselves up and stick your noses in the air as though you were the lords of creation? Very well, I shall order you. Go up to your room, get dressed, get some money for the journey and come back here.

MISS JULIE (*half-whispers*). Come with me.

JEAN. To your room? Now you're being crazy again. (*He hesitates for a moment.*) No! Go, at once! (*He takes her hand and leads her out.*)

MISS JULIE (*as she goes*). Speak kindly to me, Jean!

JEAN. An order always sounds unkind. Now you know how it feels!

JEAN, *left alone, heaves a sigh of relief, sits at the table, takes out a notebook and pencil, and makes some calculations muttering occasionally to himself.*

Dumb mime, until CHRISTINE *enters, dressed for church, with a man's dickey and white tie in her hand.*

CHRISTINE. Blessed Jesus, what a mess! What on earth have you been up to?

JEAN. Oh, it was Miss Julie – she brought the servants in. You must have been fast asleep – didn't you hear anything?

CHRISTINE. I slept like a log.

JEAN. Dressed for church already?

CHRISTINE. Yes. You promised to come with me to Communion this morning.

JEAN. So I did. And I see you've brought the uniform. O.K., then.

He sits. CHRISTINE *dresses him in his dickey and white tie. Pause.*

JEAN (*sleepily*). What's the lesson today?

CHRISTINE. Execution of John the Baptist, I expect.

JEAN. Oh God, that's a long one. Hi, you're strangling me! Oh, I'm so tired, so tired.

CHRISTINE. Well, what have you been doing, up all night? You're quite green in the face.

JEAN. Sitting here, talking with Miss Julie.

CHRISTINE. She doesn't know what's right and proper, that one.

Pause.

JEAN. I say, Christine.

CHRISTINE. Mm?

JEAN. It's strange, you know, when you think of it. Her.

CHRISTINE. What's strange?

JEAN. Everything.

Pause.

CHRISTINE (*sees the glasses, half empty, on the table*). Have you been drinking together, too?

135

JEAN. Yes.

CHRISTINE. For shame! Look me in the eyes!

JEAN. Yes?

CHRISTINE. Is it possible? Is it *possible?*

JEAN (*after a moment*). Yes.

CHRISTINE. Ugh! *That* I'd never have believed! No! Shame on you, shame!

JEAN. You aren't jealous of her, are you?

CHRISTINE. No, not of her! If it had been Clara or Sophie – then I'd have torn your eyes out. But her – no – I don't know why. Ah, but it's disgusting!

JEAN. Are you angry with her, then?

CHRISTINE. No, with you! It's a wicked thing to have done, wicked! Poor lass! No, I don't care who hears it, I don't want to stay any longer in a house where people can't respect their employers.

JEAN. Why should one respect them?

CHRISTINE. Yes, you're so clever, you tell me! But you don't want to work for people who lower themselves, do you? Eh? You lower yourself by it, that's my opinion.

JEAN. Yes, but it's a comfort for us to know they aren't any better than us.

CHRISTINE. Not to my mind. If they're no better than we are there's no point our trying to improve ourselves. And think of his lordship! Think of him and all the misery he's had in his time! No, I don't want to stay in this house any longer. Blessed Jesus! And with someone like you! If it'd been that young lawyer fellow – if it'd been a gentleman –

JEAN. What's wrong with me?

CHRISTINE. Oh, you're all right in your way, but there's a difference between people and people. No, I'll never be able to forget this. Miss Julie, who was always so proud, so cool with men – I never thought she'd go and give herself to someone – and to someone like you! She, who all but had poor Diana shot for running after the gatekeeper's pug! Yes, I'm not afraid to say it! I won't stay here any longer. On the 24th of October I go!

JEAN. And then?

CHRISTINE. Yes, since you've raised the subject, it's time you started looking round for something, seeing as we're going to get married.

JEAN. What kind of thing? I can't have a job like this once I'm married.

CHRISTINE. No, of course not. Still, you might get something as a porter, or maybe a caretaker in some government office. A bird in the hand's worth two in the bush; and there'll be a pension for your wife and children.

JEAN (*grimaces*). Yes, that's all very fine, but I don't intend to die to oblige my wife and children just yet, thank you very much. I've higher ambitions than that.

CHRISTINE. Ambitions? What about your responsibilities? Think of them.

JEAN. Oh, shut up about responsibilities, I know my duty. (*He listens towards the door.*) But we've plenty of time to think about that. Go inside now and get yourself ready, and we'll go to church.

CHRISTINE. Who's that walking about upstairs?

JEAN. I don't know. Probably Clará.

CHRISTINE (*going*). It surely can't be his lordship. He couldn't have come back without our hearing him.

JEAN (*frightened*). His lordship? No, it can't be, he'd have a rung.

CHRISTINE (*goes*). Well, God help us. I've never been mixed up in the likes of this before.

The sun has now risen and is shining on the tops of the trees in the park. Its beams move gradually until they fall at an angle through the windows. JEAN *goes to the door and makes a sign.*

MISS JULIE (*enters in travelling clothes with a small birdcage, covered with a cloth, which she places on a chair*). I'm ready now.

JEAN. Ssh! Christine is awake!

MISS JULIE (*very nervous throughout this dialogue*). Does she suspect anything?

JEAN. She knows nothing. But, my God – what a sight you look!

MISS JULIE. What's wrong – ?

JEAN. You're as white as a corpse, and – forgive me, but your face is dirty.

MISS JULIE. Let me wash, then. Here. (*She goes to the wash-basin and washes her face and hands.*) Give me a towel. Oh – the sun's rising!

JEAN. And then the Devil loses his power.

MISS JULIE. Yes, the Devil's been at work tonight. But Jean, listen. Come with me! I've got some money now.

JEAN (*doubtfully*). Enough?

MISS JULIE. Enough to start with! Come with me! I can't go alone, not today. Think – midsummer day, on a stuffy train, squashed among crowds of people staring at me – having to stand still on stations, when one longs to be flying away! No, I can't, I can't! And then – memories – memories of mid-summers in childhood, the church garlanded with birch-leaves and lilac, dinner at the long table, the family, friends – the afternoons in the park, dancing, music, flowers, games! Oh, one runs, one runs away, but memories follow in the baggage-wagon – and remorse – and guilt!

JEAN. I'll come with you – but it must be now, at once, before it's too late. Now, this minute!

MISS JULIE. Get dressed, then. (*She picks up the birdcage.*)

JEAN. No luggage, though. That'd give us away.

MISS JULIE. No, nothing. Only what we can have in the com-partment with us.

JEAN (*has taken his hat*). What have you got there? What is it?

MISS JULIE. It's only my greenfinch. I don't want to leave her.

JEAN. For heaven's sake! We can't take a birdcage with us now. You're crazy. Put that cage down.

MISS JULIE. My one memory of home – the only living thing that loves me, since Diana was unfaithful to me. Don't be cruel! Let me take her with me!

JEAN. Put that cage down, I tell you. And don't talk so loud, Christine will hear us.

MISS JULIE. No I won't leave her for strangers to have. I'd rather you killed her.

JEAN. Bring the little beast here then, and I will.

MISS JULIE. All right – but don't hurt her. Don't – no, I can....

JEAN. Bring it here. I can.

MISS JULIE (*takes the bird out of its cage and kisses it*). Ah, poor little Serina, are you going to die now and leave your mistress?

JEAN. Please don't make a scene. Your life and your happiness are at stake. Here, quickly! (*He snatches the bird from her, takes it to the chopping block and picks up the kitchen axe. MISS JULIE turns away.*) You ought to have learned how to wring chickens' necks instead of how to fire a pistol. (*He brings down the axe.*) Then you wouldn't have been frightened of a drop of blood.

MISS JULIE (*screams*). Kill me too! Kill me! You, who can slaughter an innocent creature without a tremor! Oh, I hate and detest you! There is blood between us now! I curse the moment I set eyes on you, I curse the moment I was conceived in my mother's womb!

JEAN. What's the good of cursing? Come!

MISS JULIE (*goes towards the chopping block, as though drawn against her will*). No, I don't want to go yet. I can't – I must see – ssh! There's a carriage outside! (*She listens, but keeps her eyes fixed all the while on the chopping block and the axe.*) Do you think I can't bear the sight of blood? You think I'm so weak – oh, I should like to see your blood, your brains, on a chopping block – I'd like to see all your sex swimming in a lake of blood – I think I could drink from your skull, I'd like to bathe my feet in your guts, I could eat your heart, roasted! You think I'm weak – you think I loved you, because my womb wanted your seed, you think I want to carry your embryo under my heart and feed it with my blood, bear your child and take your name! By the way, what is your surname! I've never heard it – you probably haven't any. I'd have to be 'Mrs Kitchen-boy', or 'Mrs Lavatory man' – you dog, who wear my collar, you lackey who carry my crest on your buttons – am I to share with my own cook, compete with a scullery slut? Oh, oh, oh! You think I'm a coward and want to run away? No, now I shall stay. Let the storm break! My father will come home – find his desk broken open – his money gone! He'll ring – this bell – twice, for his lackey – then he'll send for the police – and I shall tell everything. Everything. Oh, it'll be good to end it all – if only it could be the end. And then he'll have a stroke and die. Then we shall all be finished, and there'll be peace – peace – eternal rest! And the coat of arms will be broken over the coffin – the title extinct – and the lackey's line will be carried on in an orphanage, win laurels in the gutter, and end in a prison!

JEAN. That's the blue blood talking! Bravo, Miss Julie! Just give the miller a rest, now – !

CHRISTINE *enters, dressed for church, with a prayer-book in her hand.* MISS JULIE *runs towards her and falls into her arms, as though seeking shelter.*

MISS JULIE. Help me, Christine! Help me against this man!

CHRISTINE (*motionless, cold*). What kind of a spectacle's this on a Sunday morning? (*She looks at the chopping block.*) And what a pigsty you've made here. What does all this mean? I never heard such shouting and bawling.

MISS JULIE. Christine! Christine, listen to me and I'll explain everything.

JEAN (*somewhat timid and embarrassed*). While you ladies discuss the matter, I'll go inside and shave. (*He slips out right.*)

MISS JULIE. You must try to understand! You must listen to me!

CHRISTINE. No, this kind of thing I don't understand. Where are you going in those clothes? And what's he doing with his hat on – eh? – eh?

MISS JULIE. Listen to me, Christine. Listen, and I'll explain everything –

CHRISTINE. I don't want to know anything –

MISS JULIE. You must listen to me –

CHRISTINE. About what? What you've done with Jean? That doesn't bother me – that's between you and him. But if you're thinking of trying to fool him into running away, we'll soon put a stop to that.

MISS JULIE (*very nervous*). Now try to be calm, Christine, and listen to me. I can't stay here, and Jean can't stay here – so we have to go –

CHRISTINE. Hm, hm!

MISS JULIE (*becoming brighter*). Listen, I've just had an idea – why don't we all three go away – abroad – to Switzerland – and start a hotel together – I've money, you see – and Jean and I could run it – and you, I thought you might take charge of the kitchen – isn't that a good idea? Say yes, now! And come with us, and then everything'll be settled! Say yes, now!

CHRISTINE (*coldly, thoughtfully*). Hm, hm!

MISS JULIE (*speaks very rapidly*). You've never been abroad, Christine – you must get away from here and see the world. You've no idea what fun it is to travel by train – new people all the time – new countries – we'll go through Hamburg and look at the zoo – you'll like that – and then we'll go to the theatre and listen to the opera – and when we get to Munich there'll be all the museums, Christine, and Rubens and Raphael, those great painters, you know – you've heard of Munich – where King Ludwig lived, you know, the King who went mad. And we'll see his palaces – they've still got palaces there, just like in the fairy tales – and from there it isn't far to Switzerland – and the Alps, Christine – fancy, the Alps, with snow on them in the middle of summer – and oranges grow there, and laurel trees that are green all the year round –

JEAN *can be seen in the wings right, whetting his razor on a strop which he holds between his teeth and his left hand. He listens contentedly to what is being said, every now and then nodding his approval.*

MISS JULIE (*more rapidly still*). And we'll start a hotel there – I'll sit at the desk while Jean stands in the doorway and receives the guests – I'll go out and do the shopping – and write the letters – oh Christine, what a life it'll be! The trains will whistle, and then the buses'll arrive, and bells will ring on all the floors and in the restaurant – and I'll write out the bills – and salt them, too – you can't imagine how timid tourists are when they have to pay the bill! And you – you'll be in charge of the kitchen – you won't have to do any cooking yourself, of course – and you'll wear fine clothes, for the guests to see you in – and you, with your looks, I'm not flattering you, Christine, you'll get yourself a husband one fine day, a rich Englishman, you'll see – English people are so easy to – (*slowing down*) – catch – and we'll become rich – and build ourselves a villa on Lake Como – it rains there sometimes, of course, but – (*slows right down*) – the sun must shine there too, sometimes – though it looks dark – and – so – if it doesn't we can come home again – back to – (*Pause.*) Back here – or somewhere –

CHRISTINE. Now listen. Do you believe all this?

MISS JULIE (*crushed*). Do I believe it?

CHRISTINE. Yes.

MISS JULIE (*wearily*). I don't know. I don't believe in anything any longer. (*She falls on to the bench and puts her head on the table between her hands.*) Nothing. Nothing at all.

CHRISTINE (*turns right to where* JEAN *is standing*). So! You were thinking of running away!

JEAN (*crestfallen, puts his razor down on the table*). Running away? Oh now, that's exaggerating. You heard Miss Julie's plan and although she's tired now after being up all night I think it's a very practical proposition.

CHRISTINE. Listen to him! Did you expect me to act as cook to that – ?

JEAN (*sharply*). Kindly express yourself respectfully when you refer to your mistress. Understand?

CHRISTINE. Mistress!

JEAN. Yes.

CHRISTINE. Listen to him, listen to him!

JEAN. Yes, listen to me, and talk a little less. Miss Julie is your mistress, and what you despise in her you should despise in yourself too.

CHRISTINE. I've always had sufficient respect for myself –

JEAN. To be able to turn up your nose at others.

CHRISTINE. To stop me from demeaning myself. You tell me when you've seen his lordship's cook mucking around with the groom or the pigman! Just you tell me!

142

JEAN. Yes, you managed to get hold of a gentleman for yourself. You were lucky.

CHRISTINE. Yes, a gentleman who sells his lordship's oats, which he steals from the stables –

JEAN. You should talk! You take a percentage on all the groceries, and a rake-off from the butcher –

CHRISTINE. What!

JEAN. And you say you can't respect your employers! You, you, you!

CHRISTINE. Are you coming with me to church now? You need a good sermon after what you've done.

JEAN. No, I'm not going to church today. You can go by yourself, and confess what you've been up to.

CHRISTINE. Yes, I will, and I'll come home with my sins forgiven, and yours too. The blessed Saviour suffered and died on the cross for all our sins, and if we turn to Him with a loyal and humble heart He'll take all our sins upon Him.

JEAN. Including the groceries?

MISS JULIE. Do you believe that, Christine?

CHRISTINE. With all my heart, as surely as I stand here. I learned it as a child, Miss Julie, and I've believed it ever since. And where the sin is exceeding great, there His mercy shall overflow.

MISS JULIE. Oh, if only I had your faith! Oh, if – !

CHRISTINE. Ah, but you can't have that except by God's special grace, and that isn't granted to everyone –

MISS JULIE. Who has it, then?

CHRISTINE. That's God's great secret, Miss Julie. And the Lord's no respecter of persons. There shall the last be first –

MISS JULIE. Then He has respect for the last?

CHRISTINE (continues). And it is easier for a camel to pass through the eye of a needle than for a rich man to enter the Kingdom of Heaven. That's how it is, Miss Julie. Well, I'll be going – and as I pass the stable I'll tell the groom not to let any of the horses be taken out before his lordship comes home, just in case. Goodbye. (She goes.)

JEAN. Damned bitch! And all for a greenfinch!

MISS JULIE (*dully*). Never mind the greenfinch. Can you see any way out of this, any end to it?

JEAN (*thinks*). No.

MISS JULIE. What would you do in my place?

JEAN. In your place? Wait, now. If I was a lady – of noble birth – who'd fallen – ? I don't know. Yes. I do know.

MISS JULIE (*picks up the razor and makes a gesture*). This?

JEAN. Yes. But *I* wouldn't do it, mind. There's a difference between us.

MISS JULIE. Because you're a man and I am a woman? What difference does that make?

JEAN. The difference – between a man and a woman.

MISS JULIE (*holding the razor*). I want to do it – but I can't. My father couldn't do it, either, the time he should have.

JEAN. No, he was right. He had to be revenged first.

MISS JULIE. And now my mother will be revenged again, through me.

JEAN. Have you never loved your father, Miss Julie?

MISS JULIE. Yes – enormously – but I've hated him too. I must have done so without realizing it. But it was he who brought me up to despise my own sex, made me half woman and half man. Who is to blame for what has happened – my father, my mother, myself? Myself? I have no self. I haven't a thought I didn't get from my father, not an emotion I didn't get from my mother – and this last idea – that all people are equal – I got that from him, my fiancé whom I called a wretched little fool because of it. How can the blame be mine, then? Put it all on to Jesus, as Christine did – no, I'm too proud to do that, and too clever – thanks to my learned father. And that about a rich person not being able to get into heaven, that's a lie, and Christine has money in the savings bank so she won't get there either. Whose fault is it all? What does it matter to us whose fault it is? I shall have to bear the blame, carry the consequences –

JEAN. Yes, but –

There are two sharp rings on the bell. MISS JULIE *jumps up.* JEAN *changes his coat.*

JEAN. His lordship's home! Good God, do you suppose Christine – ? (*Goes to the speaking tube, knocks on it, and listens.*)

MISS JULIE. Has he been to his desk?

JEAN. It's Jean, milord. (*He listens. The audience cannot hear what is said to him.*) Yes, milord. (*He listens.*) Yes, milord. Immediately. (*He listens.*) At once, milord. (*Listens.*) Very good, my lord. In half an hour.

MISS JULIE (*desperately frightened*). What does he say? For God's sake, what does he say?

JEAN. He wants his boots and his coffee in half an hour.

MISS JULIE. In half an hour, then – ! Oh, I'm so tired! I can't feel anything, I can't repent, can't run away, can't stay, can't live – can't die. Help me! Order me, and I'll obey you like a dog. Do me this last service, save my honour, save his name! You know what I ought to will myself to do, but I can't. Will me to, Jean, order me!

JEAN. I don't know – now I can't either – I don't understand – it's just as though this coat made me – I *can't* order you – and now, since his lordship spoke to me – I can't explain it properly, but – oh, it's this damned lackey that sits on my back – I think if his lordship came down now and ordered me to cut my throat, I'd do it on the spot.

MISS JULIE. Then pretend that you are he, and I am you. You acted so well just now, when you went down on your knees – then you were an aristocrat – or – haven't you ever been to the theatre and seen a hypnotist? (JEAN *nods.*) He says to his subject: 'Take the broom!', and he takes it, He says: 'Sweep!' and he sweeps –

JEAN. But the subject has to be asleep.

MISS JULIE (*in an ecstasy*). I am already asleep – the whole room is like smoke around me – and you look like an iron stove – which resembles a man dressed in black, with a tall hat – and your eyes shine like coals, when the fire is dying – and your face is a white smear, like ash – (*The sun's rays have now reached the floor and are shining on* JEAN.) It's so warm and good – ! (*She rubs her hands as though warming them before a fire.*) And so bright – and so peaceful – !

JEAN (*takes the razor and places it in her hand*). Here's the broom.

Go now – while it's light – out to the barn – and – (*He whispers in her ear.*)

MISS JULIE (*awake*). Thank you. Now I am going to rest. But just tell me this – those who are first – they too can receive grace? Say it to me – even if you don't believe it.

JEAN. Those who are first? No, I can't! But, wait – Miss Julie – now I see it! You are no longer among the first. You are – among the last!

MISS JULIE. That's true. I am among the last of all. I am the last. Oh! But now I can't go! Tell me once more – say I must go!

JEAN. No, now I can't either. I can't!

MISS JULIE. And the first shall be last.

JEAN. Don't think, don't think! You take all my strength from me, you make me a coward. What? I thought the bell moved! No. Shall we stuff paper in it? To be so afraid of a bell! Yes, but it isn't only a bell – there's someone sitting behind it – a hand sets it in motion – and something else sets the hand in motion – you've only got to close your ears, close your ears! Yes, but now he's ringing louder! He'll ring till someone answers – and then it'll be too late. The police will come – and then – !

Two loud rings on the bell

JEAN (*cringes, then straightens himself up*). It's horrible. But it's the only possible ending. Go!

MISS JULIE *walks firmly out through the door.*

The Ghost Sonata

A CHAMBER PLAY
(1907)

Introduction to
The Ghost Sonata

Strindberg wrote *The Ghost Sonata* in February–March 1907, immediately after *Storm* and *The Burnt House*. It was the third of the 'chamber plays' composed for his Intimate Theatre, which he was to open that November; he completed the three of them in less than ten weeks.

He was living alone in the apartment in Stockholm which he had previously shared with his third wife Harriet Bosse and their daughter, Anne-Marie. He had recently had a recurrence of psoriasis, the humiliating and painful skin disease which had discomfited him in Paris during his scientific experiments, and the slightest contact with anything, even a pen, made his hands bleed. According to his sister Anna, the first symptoms of the stomach cancer which was to kill him five years later had also manifested themselves.[1] He thus wrote *The Ghost Sonata* in a state of almost permanent physical pain. This made him more than usually impossible to live with, and six servants left him within forty days, including, two days before he finished the play, his cook. It is not surprising that *The Ghost Sonata*, and *The Pelican* which followed it, are so much crueller and more bitter than *Storm*, which he wrote in loneliness, but in apparent resignation.

The Ghost Sonata marks a return to that mood of cynicism and disillusionment with the world of the living which we find so often in his earlier work. In 1905 he had written: 'Life is so horribly ugly, we human beings so utterly evil, that if a writer were to portray *everything* he saw and heard no one could bear to read it. There are things which I remember having seen and heard in good, respectable and well-liked people, but which I have blotted out from my mind because I could not bring myself to speak of them and do not wish to remember them.

[1] In the original draft of the play, the Daughter's illness is identified as being cancer of the womb.

Breeding and education are only masks to hide our bestiality, and virtue is a sham. The best we can hope for is to conceal our wretchedness. Life is so cynical that only a swine can be happy in it; and any man who sees beauty in life's ugliness *is* a swine! Life is a punishment. A hell. For some a purgatory, for none a paradise. We are compelled to commit evil and to torment our fellow mortals.'

On 27 March 1907 he wrote to his German translator, Emil Schering: 'I am sending you today a second Chamber Play (opus 3), called *A* [sic] *Ghost Sonata* (subtitled *Kama-Loka*, though that needn't be printed). It is horrifying like life, when the veil falls from our eyes and we see things as they are. It has shape and content, the wisdom that comes with age, as our knowledge increases and we learn to understand. This is how "The Weaver" weaves men's destinies; secrets like these are to be found in *every* home. People are too proud to admit it; most of them boast of their imagined luck, and hide their misery. The Colonel acts out his private comedy to the end; illusion (Maya) has become reality to him – the Mummy awakens first, one cannot wake the others. . . . I have suffered as though in Kama-Loka[1] (Scheol) during the writing of it and my hands have bled (literally). What has saved my soul from darkness during this work has been my religion (= contact with the hereafter). Hope of a better life to come; the firm conviction that we live in a world of madness and delusion (illusion) from which we must fight our way free. For me things have become brighter, and I have written with the feeling that this is my "Last Sonata!"'

A week later, he wrote again to Schering: 'Now I am assuredly entering into something new. I long for the light, have always done so, but have not found it. Is it the end that is approaching? I don't know, but I feel that it is so. Life is, as it were squeezing me out, or driving me out, and I have long since rested all my hopes on "the other side", with which I am in contact (through Swedenborg). A feeling has also come over

[1] Kama-Loka – 'a kind of ghost or dream world through which mortals, or some mortals, have to wander before they enter the peace of death's kingdom' (Olle Holmberg).

me that I have completed my work, that I have nothing more to say. My whole life often seems to me to have been planned like a play, so that I might both suffer and depict suffering.'

While he was writing *The Ghost Sonata*, preparations were under way for the first production of *A Dream Play* that April, and this may partly explain why he returned to a certain degree to the technique of the earlier play and of *To Damascus*. In his preface to *A Dream Play*, Strindberg had written: 'In this dream play, the author has, as in his former dream play, *To Damascus*, attempted to imitate the inconsequent yet transparently logical shape of a dream. Everything can happen, everything is possible and probable. Time and place do not exist; on an insignificant basis of reality the imagination spins, weaving new patterns; a mixture of memories, experiences, free fancies, incongruities and improvizations. The characters split, double, multiply, evaporate, condense, disperse, assemble. But one consciousness rules over them all, that of the dreamer; for him there are no secrets, no illogicalities, no scruples, no laws. He neither acquits nor condemns, but merely relates; and, just as a dream is more often painful than happy, so an undertone of melancholy and of pity for all mortal beings accompanies this flickering tale.'

The characters in *The Ghost Sonata* are based on people whom Strindberg saw in his respectable suburb of Östermalm. On his walks he sometimes came across a rich old man in a wheel-chair who ostentatiously dispensed charity to beggars. Through the window of a house he observed a youngish man playing cards with three old people who looked like mummies. The Daughter and the Student may have been modelled on his own daughter, Greta, and her fiancé, Henry Philp, to whom she had become engaged the previous December; he was very fond of both these young people, who seemed untouched by evil in an evil world.[1] The Mummy and the Colonel appear to have been based, like the two protagonists in *The Dance of Death*, on his sister Anna and her husband, Hugo Philp (the parents of Henry Philp); they had been kind to Strindberg and, as was his

[1] Greta Strindberg was killed in a railway accident in the same year that her father died (1912) at the age of thirty-one.

habit, he had turned violently against them. In 1900 Hugo
Philp had put a 'von' before his name, which may have given
Strindberg the idea of making the Colonel falsely claim to be
a nobleman. The soya or colorite bottle carried by the Cook
held some particular significance for Strindberg, for he specifi-
cally commanded Schering not to omit it from his translation.
'N.B.! Don't forget the soya bottle, the colorite which I have
had to put up with for thirteen days; I have been eating coloured water', he wrote to him on 7 April 1907. Presumably his
cook had given up the struggle. The Japanese screen stood in
the Philps' home; and the idea of a death screen was given him
by a niece, who was a hospital nurse and told him of the pro-
cedure in a ward when a patient dies. Böcklin's *Island of the
Dead*, mentioned in the final stage direction, was one of Strindberg's favourite paintings, and when the Intimate Theatre
opened that winter reproductions of it and of the same painter's
Island of the Living hung on either side of the proscenium arch.

The Ghost Sonata was first acted at the Intimate Theatre on
21 January 1908, and was, like the other three chamber plays
which preceded it, *Storm*, *The Burnt House* and *The Pelican*,
violently condemned by the critics. As with *Storm*, it was
Max Reinhardt who first revealed the play's possibilities
when he staged it in 1916 in Berlin, a production the fame
of which spread to many countries even in that dark time. The
same year he took his production to Gothenburg and Stockholm, where it created a considerable sensation. Paul Wegener
played Hummel and Gertrud Eysoldt the Mummy. In 1917
the play was produced in Munich, in 1920 in Copenhagen
(with Reinhardt as guest producer), in 1921 in Oslo and in 1922
in Vienna. In 1924, at the instigation of Eugene O'Neill, the
Provincetown Players presented *The Ghost Sonata* in New
York; in 1925 it was successfully staged in Rome at Bragaglia's
experimental theatre; and in 1926 it at last reached England,
when J. B. Fagan presented it at the Oxford Playhouse. The
following year Fagan brought his production to the Globe
Theatre in London for two matinées; some critics, including
James Agate, were impressed, but the general public reaction
was one of bewilderment.

The Ghost Sonata has not been professionally staged in England since 1927 (although there have been numerous performances by amateurs, especially at the universities), but on 16 March 1962 it was televised by the B.B.C. in a production by Stuart Burge, which, as several critics remarked, was probably watched by more people than had seen the play during the previous fifty-five years of its existence. Robert Helpmann played Hummel, Beatrix Lehmann the Mummy and Jeremy Brett the Student, and it is a measure of the development of theatrical taste that the public reaction from this huge audience was predominantly favourable. It was even more positive when the play was newly directed on BBC television on 23 March 1980 by Philip Saville, with Donald Pleasance as Hummel, Lila Kedrova as the Mummy and Clive Arrindell as the Student.

Strindberg wrote seven plays after *The Ghost Sonata*, but none of them can be reckoned among his best. His Intimate Theatre finally failed and closed in 1910, and he devoted the last three years of his life to writing pamphlets on politics, sociology and philology. He died of stomach cancer on 14 May 1912, aged sixty-three.

The Ghost Sonata

This translation of *The Ghost Sonata* was commissioned by the British Broadcasting Corporation and was first performed on B.B.C. Television on 16 March 1962. The cast was:

THE OLD MAN	Robert Helpmann
THE STUDENT	Jeremy Brett
THE MILKMAID, a vision	Linda Gardner
THE CARETAKER'S WIFE	Miki Iveria
THE DEAD MAN, a Consul	George McGrath
THE DARK LADY, daughter to the Caretaker's Wife by the Dead Man	Yvonne Coulette
THE COLONEL	William Mervyn
THE MUMMY, wife to the Colonel	Beatrix Lehmann
THE 'COLONEL'S DAUGHTER', in reality the Old Man's daughter	Ann Bell
THE NOBLEMAN, known as BARON SKANSKORG, engaged to the Caretaker's Daughter	Arthur Lawrence
JOHANSSON, servant to the Old Man	Thomas Heathcote
BENGTSSON, footman to the Colonel	John Kidd
THE FIANCÉE, a white-haired old lady, formerly engaged to the Old Man	Jane Eccles
THE COOK	Anna Wing
A MAIDSERVANT	Mary McMillen

Designed by Clifford Hatts
Directed by Stuart Burge

The ground floor and first floor of a fashionable house. Only a corner of it is visible. The ground floor ends in a circular drawing-room, the first floor in a balcony with a flagstaff.

As the blinds are raised in the drawing-room they reveal through the open windows a white marble statue of a young woman, surrounded by palms which are bathed in bright sunlight. In the window to the left stand vases of hyacinths, blue, white and pink.

Over the railing of the balcony, at the corner of the first floor, hangs a blue silk eiderdown, with two white pillows. The windows to the left are draped with white sheets. It is a clear Sunday morning.

Downstage, in front of the house, is a green bench. Downstage right, a public fountain. To the left is a pillar, with posters pasted round it.

Upstage left is the front entrance to the house. Through it we can see the staircase, which is of white marble, with banisters of mahogany and brass. On the pavement outside, laurels in tubs stand on either side of the door.

The corner of the house which contains the round drawing-room also looks on to a side street which leads upstage.

To the left of the entrance, on the ground floor, is a window with a mirror outside it set at an angle.

As the curtain rises, the bells of several churches can be heard pealing in the distance.

The doors of the house are open. A WOMAN *dressed in dark clothes is standing motionless on the staircase. The* CARETAKER'S WIFE *is cleaning the front step; then she polishes the brass on the front door, and waters the laurels.*

In a wheel chair by the pillar, the OLD MAN *sits reading the paper. He has white hair, a white beard, and spectacles.*

The MILKMAID *enters from the left, carrying bottles in a wire basket. She is in summer clothes, with brown shoes, black stockings and a white cap. She takes off the cap and hangs it on the fountain, wipes the sweat from her forehead, drinks from the cup, washes her hands and arranges her hair, using the water as a mirror.*

A steamship's bell rings, and the bass notes of an organ in a nearby church intermittently pierce the silence.

After a few moments of this silence, when the MILKMAID *has finished her toilet, the* STUDENT *enters from the left, sleepless and unshaven. He goes straight to the fountain.*

Pause.

STUDENT. May I have the cup?

THE MILKMAID *hugs the cup to her.*

You've finished with it, haven't you?

THE MILKMAID *looks at him, frightened.*

OLD MAN (*to himself*). Who's he talking to? I can't see anyone. Is he mad? (*He continues to watch them in great amazement.*)

STUDENT. What are you staring at? Am I so repulsive? Oh, I see. I haven't slept all night, so of course you think I've been dissipating. (*She still stares at him with the same expression.*) Drinking punch, hm? Does my breath smell of punch? (*Her expression remains unchanged.*) I haven't shaved – oh, I know. Give me a drink of water, girl – I've earned it. (*Pause.*) Oh, very well. I suppose I'll have to tell you. I've been bandaging wounds all night, and tending the injured; I was there when the house collapsed yesterday evening. Now you know.

THE MILKMAID *rinses the cup and gives him a drink.*

Thank you.

THE MILKMAID *does not move.*

(*Slowly.*) Will you do me a service? (*Pause.*) It's like this. My eyes are swollen, as you can see, but I daren't touch them with my hands because I've been fingering open wounds and dead bodies. Will you take this handkerchief, moisten it in the clean water and bathe my eyes? Will you do that?

158

Will you be my Good Samaritan? (*She hesitates, but does as he asks.*) Thank you, dear friend. (*Takes out his purse. She makes a gesture of refusal.*) Oh – forgive me for being so thoughtless – I'm not really awake –

OLD MAN (*to the* STUDENT). Pardon my addressing you, but did I hear you say you witnessed that accident last night? I've just been reading about it in the paper –

STUDENT. Oh, have they got hold of it already?

OLD MAN. Yes, the whole story's here. And your photograph; but they regret they were unable to discover the name of the brilliant young student who –

STUDENT (*looks at the paper*). Really? That's me! Well, well.

OLD MAN. Whom were you talking to just now?

STUDENT. Didn't you see her?

Pause.

OLD MAN. Would it be impertinent of me to ask – to be allowed the honour of knowing – your name?

STUDENT. What'd be the point? I don't want any publicity; once you become famous people start saying foul things about you. Depreciation's become a fine art nowadays. Anyway, I'm not looking for any reward –

OLD MAN. You are rich?

STUDENT. Quite the contrary. I'm ab-absolutely penniless.

OLD MAN. Wait a moment! I seem to know that voice. When I was young I had a friend who couldn't say absinthe, he always said ab-absinthe. He's the only person I've ever come across with that particular stammer. And now you! I wonder if you could possibly be any relation to a wholesale merchant of the name of Arkenholz?

STUDENT. He was my father.

OLD MAN. The ways of fate are strange. I saw you once, when you were a little child – under very painful circumstances –

STUDENT. Yes. I'm said to have been born into this world in the home of a bankrupt.

OLD MAN. Precisely.

STUDENT. Perhaps I may ask your name?

OLD MAN. My name is Hummel.

STUDENT. Are *you* – ? Yes – now I remember –

OLD MAN. You've often heard my name mentioned by your family?

STUDENT. Yes.

OLD MAN. Mentioned, I dare say, with a certain – distaste?

THE STUDENT *is silent*.

Oh, yes – I can imagine! I've no doubt they told you it was I who ruined your father? People who ruin themselves by idiotic speculation always swear they've been ruined by the one man they failed to fool. (*Pause.*) The truth of the matter is that your father swindled me out of seventeen thousand crowns – a sum which at the time represented my entire savings.

STUDENT. It's strange how a story can exist in two such different versions.

OLD MAN. You think I'm not telling you the truth.

STUDENT. What else am I to think? My father never lied?

OLD MAN. True, true. One's own father never lies. But I am a father, too; so –

STUDENT. What are you trying to tell me?

OLD MAN. I saved your father from complete destitution, and he rewarded me with hatred – the dreadful hatred of a man tied to another by the knot of gratitude. He taught his family to spit on my name.

STUDENT. Perhaps you made him ungrateful by poisoning your charity with unnecessary humiliations?

OLD MAN. All charity is humiliating, my dear sir.

STUDENT. What do you want from me?

OLD MAN. Oh, not money. If you would just perform one or two trivial services for me, I shall think myself well repaid. I am, as you see, a cripple. Some say it is my own fault, others blame my parents. I prefer to believe that life itself is to blame; she's a cunning snarer; sidestep one pit and you walk straight into the next. Be that as it may, I cannot run up stairs or pull bell-ropes, and therefore I say to you: 'Please help me.'

STUDENT. What can I do?

OLD MAN. First of all, push my chair so that I can read these posters. I want to see what they're playing tonight at the theatre —

STUDENT (*pushes the wheel chair*). Haven't you a servant?

OLD MAN. Yes, but he's gone on an errand. He'll be back soon. So you're a medical student, are you?

STUDENT. No, I'm studying languages. I haven't really decided yet what I'm going to be —

OLD MAN. Ah-ha! Are you any good at arithmetic?

STUDENT. I know a little.

OLD MAN. Good! Would you like a job?

STUDENT. Yes. Why not?

OLD MAN. Excellent! (*Reads one of the posters.*) They're giving a matinée this afternoon of *The Valkyrie*. The Colonel'll be there with his daughter. He always sits at the end of the sixth row. I'll put you beside them. Go into that telephone kiosk, will you, and book a ticket for seat number 82 in the sixth row?

STUDENT. You want me to go the the opera this afternoon?

OLD MAN. Yes. Just do as I tell you and you'll be well rewarded. I want you to be happy, to find wealth and honour. By tomorrow your gallant deeds of rescue will be in every mouth, and your name will have a considerable market value —

STUDENT (*goes towards the telephone kiosk*). This is a strange adventure.

OLD MAN. Are you a gambler?

STUDENT. Yes. That's my tragedy.

OLD MAN. It shall be your fortune. Go along and do your telephoning.

He reads his newspaper. The WOMAN *dressed in dark clothes has come out on to the pavement and is talking to the* CARETAKER'S WIFE. *The* OLD MAN *listens, but the audience cannot hear what they say. The* STUDENT *returns.*

OLD MAN. Have you done it?

STUDENT. Yes.

OLD MAN. You see that house?

161

STUDENT. Yes. I've noticed it before. I was walking past it yesterday, as the sun was shining in its windows. I thought of all the beauty and luxury there must be inside, and said to my companion: 'If only one had an apartment there, four floors up, with a beautiful young wife, two pretty children and a private income of 20,000 crowns a year.'

OLD MAN. You said that, did you, did you indeed? Well, now; I love this house, too –

STUDENT. You speculate in houses?

OLD MAN. Mm – yes. But not the way you mean –

STUDENT. You know the people who live there?

OLD MAN. Every one of them. When you live to be as old as I am, you know everyone, who their fathers were and their forefathers, and you find you're related to all of them in some way or other. I'm eighty; but no-one knows me; not really – I'm interested in people's destinies –

The blind in the round drawing-room is raised. The COLONEL *is seen within, dressed in mufti. After looking at the thermometer, he turns back into the room and stops in front of the marble statue.*

OLD MAN. Look, there's the Colonel. You'll be sitting next to him this afternoon –

STUDENT. Is that – the Colonel? I don't understand what any of this means – it's like a fairy tale –

OLD MAN. My whole life is a book of fairy tales, my dear sir; and although each tale is different, a single thread links them, there is a *leitmotif* that recurs continually –

STUDENT. Whom does the marble statue represent?

OLD MAN. His wife, of course.

STUDENT. Was she so beautiful?

OLD MAN. Mm – yes. Yes.

STUDENT. Tell me.

OLD MAN. Ah, my dear boy, we must not judge our fellow mortals. If I were to tell you that he struck her, that she left him, that she came back to him, and re-married him, and that she now sits in there in the shape of a mummy, worshipping her own statue, you would think I was mad.

STUDENT. I don't understand.

OLD MAN. I didn't suppose you would. Then we have the hyacinth window. That's where his daughter lives. She's out riding, but she'll be home soon –

STUDENT. Who is the dark lady talking to the caretaker's wife?

OLD MAN. Well, that's a bit complicated. It's to do with the dead man upstairs – up there, where you can see the white sheets –

STUDENT. Who was he?

OLD MAN. A human being, like us; but vain – vain. If you were a Sunday child, in a few minutes you would see him come out through the door to look at the consulate flag flying at half-mast. He was a consul, and loved crowns and lions, plumed hats and coloured ribbons –

STUDENT. Sunday child, you said. They say I was born on a Sunday –

OLD MAN. You don't say! Were you really? I might have guessed it from the colour of your eyes. Then you can see what others cannot see. Have you noticed that?

STUDENT. I don't know what other people can see, but sometimes – well, I'd rather not talk about it.

OLD MAN. I knew it. Come on, you can tell me. I understand about these things –

STUDENT. Well – yesterday, for example. I felt myself drawn to that quite ordinary little street in which, in a few minutes, a house was to collapse. I walked down it and stopped in front of this building – I'd never seen it before. Then I noticed a crack in the wall and heard the floorboards snapping. I ran forward and snatched hold of a child who was walking close by the wall. The next moment, the house collapsed. I was safe. But in my arms, where I thought I was holding the child, there was nothing.

OLD MAN. Extraordinary. I guessed as much. But tell me something. Why were you gesticulating like that at the fountain just now? And why were you talking to yourself?

STUDENT. Didn't you see the milkmaid?

OLD MAN (recoils). Milkmaid?

STUDENT. Yes, the one who gave me the cup?

OLD MAN. Ah-ha? So that's how it is? Well, I can't see, but I can –

A white-haired woman sits down by the window beside the angled mirror.

OLD MAN. Look at that old woman in the window. You see her? Good. She was my fiancée once – sixty years ago. I was twenty. Don't be afraid, she doesn't recognize me. We see each other every day, but I don't feel anything, though we once vowed to be eternally true to each other. Eternally.

STUDENT. How little your generation understood of life. We don't talk to our girls like that nowadays.

OLD MAN. Forgive us, my boy, we knew no better. But can you see that this old woman was once young and beautiful?

STUDENT. No. Yes, she has an attractive glance. Though – I can't see her eyes –

The CARETAKER'S WIFE *comes out with a basket and scatters pine twigs.*[1]

OLD MAN. Ah, yes. The caretaker's wife. The dark lady over there is her daughter, by the dead man. That's how her husband got the job as caretaker. But the dark lady has a lover; a nobleman, with great expectations. He's getting divorced from his wife – she's giving him a fine house so as to be rid of him. This noble lover is son-in-law to the dead man – you can see his bedclothes being aired up there on the balcony. Complicated, isn't it?

STUDENT. Confoundedly complicated.

OLD MAN. Yes; it's a complicated house, inside and out. Yet it looks quite ordinary, doesn't it?

STUDENT. But who was the dead man, then?

OLD MAN. You asked me just now, and I told you. If you could see round the corner to the back entrance, you'd see a crowd of paupers whom he used to help. When he felt inclined –

STUDENT. He was a kind man, then?

OLD MAN. Sometimes.

STUDENT. Not always?

---

[1] A custom in Sweden when someone has died.

OLD MAN. No. People are like that. Now, my dear sir, move my chair a little so that it gets the sun. I'm so horribly cold; when one can't move, the blood stiffens. I'm going to die soon, I know that, but there are one or two things I've got to do before I go. Take my hand, feel how cold I am.

STUDENT (*recoils*). It's horrible!

OLD MAN. Don't leave me. I'm tired, I'm lonely, but I haven't always been like this, you know. I've an interminably long life behind me – oh, interminably long. I've made people unhappy, and people have made me unhappy – I suppose the one cancels out the other – but before I die I want to see you happy. Our destinies are wedded – through your father – and in other ways, too.

STUDENT. Let go of my hand, you're draining my strength, you're freezing me. What do you want?

OLD MAN. Be patient. You will see and understand. Here comes the young lady.

STUDENT. The Colonel's daughter?

OLD MAN. Yes! His daughter! Look at her! Did you ever see such a masterpiece?

STUDENT. She's like the marble statue in there.

OLD MAN. That's her mother.

STUDENT. Yes – you're right! I never saw such a woman – of woman born. Happy the man who leads her to the altar and to his home!

OLD MAN. Ah – you see it, then? Not everyone appreciates her beauty. Good, good; it is written so.

The DAUGHTER *enters from the left in a fashionable English riding habit, with breeches, and walks slowly, without looking at anyone, to the door. She pauses, and says a few words to the* CARETAKER'S WIFE; *then she enters the house. The* STUDENT *puts his hand to his eyes.*

OLD MAN. Are you crying?

STUDENT. When one stands face to face with the unattainable, what else can one do but despair?

OLD MAN. I can open doors, and human hearts, if only I can find a hand to perform my will. Serve me, and you will win her.

STUDENT. Is this a pact? Must I sell my soul?

OLD MAN. Sell nothing! Listen. All my life I have taken; now
I have a longing to give. To give! But no one will take anything from me. I am rich, very rich, but I have no heirs – only
a rascal, who plagues the life out of me. Be a son to me, be
my heir while I am still alive, enjoy life so that I can watch
you enjoy it – if only from a distance.

STUDENT. What must I do?

OLD MAN. First, go and listen to *The Valkyrie*.

STUDENT. I've agreed to that. What else?

OLD MAN. Tonight you shall sit in there, in the round drawing-
room.

STUDENT. How shall I get in there?

OLD MAN. Through *The Valkyrie*!

STUDENT. Why have you chosen me as your medium? Did
you know me before?

OLD MAN. Yes, of course. I've had my eye on you for a long
time. But look up there, now – on the balcony! The maid's
hoisting the flag to half mast for the consul. Now she's
turning the bedclothes. You see the blue eiderdown? That
was made for two to sleep under. Now it serves for one.

The DAUGHTER, *who has changed her clothes, enters and waters
the hyacinths in the window.*

That's my little girl – look at her, look! She's talking to the
flowers – isn't she like a blue hyacinth herself? She's giving
them drink – just plain water, but they turn it into colour
and perfume. Here comes the Colonel with his newspaper.
He's showing her the paragraph about the accident. Now
he's pointing at your photograph! She's interested; she's
reading of your bravery. It's clouding over, what if it should
rain? I'll be in a fine pickle stuck here if Johansson doesn't
get back soon.

It clouds over and becomes dark. The OLD LADY *at the mirror
shuts her window.*

Now my fiancée's shutting her window ... seventy-nine ...
that mirror's the only one she uses, because she can't see

herself in it, only the outside world, and that from two angles
– but the world can see her, she hasn't thought of that. She's
a beautiful old lady, though. . . .

The DEAD MAN, *in his winding-sheet, emerges from the door.*

STUDENT. God Almighty, what do I see now?

OLD MAN. What do you see?

STUDENT. Can't you see? There – in the doorway! The dead
man?

OLD MAN. I see nothing. But I was expecting this. Tell me.

STUDENT. He's going out into the street. (*Pause.*) Now he's
turning his head and looking at the flag.

OLD MAN. What did I tell you? Next he'll count the wreaths:
and read the names on the cards. Woe to those whose names
he cannot find!

STUDENT. Now he's going round the corner –

OLD MAN. He's going to count the beggars at the back door.
It always looks good to have the poor at one's funeral.
'Accompanied to his grave by the blessings of the people.'
Yes, he won't have my blessing, though. Between ourselves,
he was a dreadful scoundrel –

STUDENT. But charitable –

OLD MAN. A charitable scoundrel, whose only dream in life
was to have a beautiful funeral. When he felt that the end
was near, he fleeced the estate of 50,000 crowns. Now his
daughter's living with another woman's husband, worrying
whether she'll get her inheritance. He can hear everything
we say, the rogue, and serve him right! Ah, here's Johansson.

JOHANSSON *enters from the left.*

OLD MAN. Well, what news? (JOHANSSON *speaks inaudibly.*)
Not at home? Fool! Anything on the telegraph? Nothing.
Go on. Six o'clock this evening? That's good. Special
edition? With his full name? Arkenholz . . . student . . .
born . . . parents . . . Excellent! Oh, I think it's starting to
rain. What did he say? I see, I see. . . . Didn't want to. . . . ?
Well he must. . . . Here comes the noble lover. Push me
round the corner, Johansson, I want to hear what the beggars

are saying. Arkenholz, wait for me here; you understand?
Hurry, hurry!

JOHANSSON *pushes the wheel-chair round the corner. The*
STUDENT *remains where he is, watching the* DAUGHTER, *who
is now raking the earth in the flowerpots.*

NOBLEMAN (*in mourning, addresses the* DARK LADY, *who has
come out on to the pavement.*) Well, what can we do about it?
We'll just have to wait.

LADY. I cannot wait.

NOBLEMAN. Is that so? Better leave town, then.

DARK LADY. I don't want to do that.

NOBLEMAN. Come over here, or they'll hear what we're
saying.

*They go over by the pillar and continue their conversation
inaudibly.*

JOHANSSON (*enters from the right and addresses the* STUDENT.)
The master says please not to forget the other matter.

STUDENT. Does your master own this house?

JOHANSSON. Yes.

STUDENT. Tell me – who is he?

JOHANSSON. Ah! He's a lot of things – and he *has* been everything.

STUDENT. Is he sane?

JOHANSSON. Depends what you mean by that. All his life he
says he's been looking for a Sunday child. Might not be true,
of course.

STUDENT. What does he want? Is he a miser?

JOHANSSON. He wants power. All day he drives round in his
chariot like the great god Thor. He looks at houses, knocks
them down, opens up streets, builds over public squares –
and he breaks into houses, too, creeps in through windows,
mucks around with people's destinies, kills his enemies, and,
never forgives. But would you believe it, sir, this little
cripple used to be a Don Juan once. Always lost his women
in the end, though.

STUDENT. Oh, why was that?

JOHANSSON. Well, he's crafty, you see. Got them to leave him once he'd tired of them. Now he's become a horse-thief – only he don't steal horses, he steals human beings. All sorts of ways. Me, now for example. He literally stole me from out of the hands of justice. I'd committed a – hm – little blunder, and he was the only one who knew about it. Well, instead of putting me inside he made me his slave. Which I do just for my food, which ain't the best –

STUDENT. What does he want to do in this house?

JOHANSSON. Ah, that I wouldn't like to say. It's all very complicated.

STUDENT. I think I'm getting out of this.

JOHANSSON. Look, the young lady's dropped her bracelet through the window.

The DAUGHTER *has dropped her bracelet through the open window. The* STUDENT *goes slowly forward, picks it up and hands it to her. She thanks him stiffly. The* STUDENT *goes back to* JOHANSSON.

JOHANSSON. Mm, so you're thinking of going? That's not so easy, once he's got his net over your head. He's afraid of nothing between earth and heaven – oh, yes, one thing. Or rather, one person –

STUDENT. Wait a moment. I think I know.

JOHANSSON. How can you?

STUDENT. I can guess. Is it – a little milkmaid?

JOHANSSON. He always turns his face away when he meets a milkcart. And he talks in his sleep – says he was once in Hamburg –

STUDENT. Can one believe that man?

JOHANSSON. You can believe him all right. Whatever he says.

STUDENT. What's he doing round the corner now?

JOHANSSON. Listening to the beggars. Drops a word – picks each brick out, grain by grain, till the house collapses. Figuratively speaking, of course. I'm an educated man, you know. Used to be a bookseller – once. You going now?

STUDENT. I don't want to seem ungrateful. This man saved my

father once, and now he's only asking a small service of me in return –

JOHANSSON. What's that?

STUDENT. He wants me to go and see *The Valkyrie*.

JOHANSSON. Can't understand that. But he's always thinking up new ideas. Look, now he's talking to the policeman. He always keeps in with the police – uses them, implicates them in his affairs, ties their hands with false hopes and promises, and all the time pumps them for information. You'll see – before the night's over he'll have nosed his way into that round room.

STUDENT. What does he want there? What is there between him and the Colonel?

JOHANSSON. Ah – I could make a guess, but I ain't sure. You'll see for yourself when you get there.

STUDENT. I shall never be admitted there.

JOHANSSON. That depends on you. Go to *The Valkyrie* –

STUDENT. You mean, then I might – ?

JOHANSSON. If that's what he's told you to do. Look at him now, riding in his war chariot! Look at the beggars drawing him in triumph! They won't get a penny for their pains – just a nod to remind them they'll get a blow-out at his funeral.

OLD MAN (*enters, standing in his wheel-chair, drawn by a beggar and followed by others*). Hail to the noble youth who, at the peril of his own life, saved many lives in yesterday's disaster. Hail, Arkenholz!

The BEGGARS *take off their caps, but do not cheer. The* DAUGHTER *waves her handkerchief at her window. The* COLONEL *stares out through his window. The* OLD WOMAN *stands up at her window. The* MAID *on the balcony hoists the flag to the top of the mast.*

OLD MAN. Clap your hands, fellow citizens! It is Sunday, but the ass at the well and the ear in the field absolve us by their toil. Although I am not a Sunday child, yet I possess the gift of prophecy, and also the gift of healing. I once summoned a drowning girl back to life. It was in Hamburg – one Sunday morning – as it might be now –

The MILKMAID *enters, seen only by the* STUDENT *and the* OLD MAN. *She stretches up her arms like a drowning person, and stares fixedly at the* OLD MAN.

OLD MAN (*sits down and cringes in terror*). Johansson, take me away! Quickly! Arkenholz, do not forget *The Valkyrie!*

STUDENT. What does all this mean?

JOHANSSON. We shall see. We shall see.

Inside the round drawing-room. Upstage, a cylindrical, white-tiled stove, with mirrors in it. A pendulum clock; candelabra. On the right is an entrance hall, with a perspective of a green room containing mahogany furniture. On the left stands the statue, shadowed by palms. There is a curtain that can be drawn to conceal it. Upstage left is the door to the hyacinth room, where the DAUGHTER *sits, reading. The* COLONEL's *back is visible as he sits writing in the green room.*

BENGTSSON, *the* COLONEL's *footman, enters from the hall dressed in livery, with* JOHANSSON, *who is wearing tails and a white cravat.*

BENGTSSON. Right, then. You do the serving, and I'll take their clothes. Ever done this kind of thing before?

JOHANSSON. I spend all day pushing his chariot, as you know, but I sometimes serve at parties of an evening. It's always been my dream to enter this house. Queer bunch, aren't they?

BENGTSSON. Uh-huh. Bit out of the ordinary.

JOHANSSON. Musical evening, or what?

BENGTSSON. No – just the usual ghost supper. That's what we call it. They sit round drinking tea, none of them utters a word – unless maybe the Colonel talks on his own. They nibble little cakes, all together. Sounds like rats in an attic.

JOHANSSON. Why do you call it the ghost supper?

BENGTSSON. Well, they look like ghosts. They've been doing this for twenty years, always the same bunch saying the same things, or keeping their traps shut for fear of making fools of themselves.

JOHANSSON. Hasn't he a wife here, too?

BENGTSSON. Yes, but she's mad. Sits in a cupboard, because her eyes can't stand the light. In here. (*Points to a door concealed in the wall.*)

JOHANSSON. In there?

BENGTSSON. Yes. I told you they're a bit out of the ordinary.

JOHANSSON. What does she look like?

BENGTSSON. Like a mummy. Care to see her? (*Opens the concealed door.*) Look, there she is.

JOHANSSON. Jesus Chr – !

MUMMY (*in the voice of a small child*). Why are you opening the door? Haven't I said it's to be kept shut!

BENGTSSON (*talking baby-talk*). Now, now, now, now. Little girlie must be good, and she'll get a sweetie. Pretty Poll!

MUMMY (*speaks like a parrot*). Pretty Poll! Is Jacob there? Funny man.

BENGTSSON. She thinks she's a parrot. Could be she is. (*To* MUMMY.) Now then, Polly, whistle for us.

The MUMMY *whistles.*

JOHANSSON. I've seen a good deal in my time, but never the likes of this.

BENGTSSON. Well, you know, when a house gets old it starts to decay, and when people sit for years in the same room torturing each other, they go off their nut. Madam here, now – quiet, Polly! – this mummy's been sitting here for forty years. Same husband, same furniture, same relatives, same friends. (*Shuts the door on the* MUMMY *again.*) As to what's gone on in this house – well, I shouldn't like to commit myself. See this statue? That's her when she was young.

JOHANSSON. My God! *This* – the mummy?

BENGTSSON. Yes. Enough to make you cry, isn't it? And that's not all. Somehow or other – imagination, maybe – she's become just like a parrot in all sorts of little ways. Can't stand cripples, for example. Or invalids. Can't even bear the sight of her own daughter, because she's ill –

JOHANSSON. The young lady? Is she ill?

BENGTSSON. Didn't you know?

JOHANSSON. No. What about the Colonel? What sort of a man's he?

BENGTSSON. You'll see.

JOHANSSON (*looks at the statue*). It's horrible. How old is – Madam – now?

BENGTSSON. No-one knows. They say that when she was thirty-five she looked nineteen, and got the Colonel to believe she was. In this very house. Know what that black Japanese screen's for, over by the chaise longue? That's called the death screen. They put it out when someone's going to die – like in a hospital –

JOHANSSON. What a horrible house! And that young student was pining his heart out to get in here, as though it was Paradise –

BENGTSSON. What student? Oh, him. The one who's coming this evening. The Colonel and his daughter met him at the opera. They both fell for him. Hm! Now it's my turn to ask you a question. Who's – er – behind him? That old boy in the wheel chair?

JOHANSSON. Yes. Yes. He coming too?

BENGTSSON. He hasn't been invited.

JOHANSSON. He'll come uninvited. If need be.

The OLD MAN *appears in the entrance lobby, wearing a long, black frock-coat and top hat. He edges silently forward on his crutches and listens.*

BENGTSSON. Real old robber, I've heard.

JOHANSSON. One of the worst.

BENGTSSON. Looks like Old Nick himself.

JOHANSSON. He's a magician, too. He can pass through closed doors –

OLD MAN (*on them, seizes* JOHANSSON *by the ear*). Villain! Beware! (*To* BENGTSSON). Tell the Colonel I have arrived.

BENGTSSON. But he's expecting guests –

OLD MAN. I know. But he's been half-expecting me; if not exactly looking forward to it.

BENGTSSON. Oh, I see. What name shall I say? Mr. Hummel?

OLD MAN. Yes.

BENGTSSON *goes through the lobby to the green room, the door of which is then closed.*

OLD MAN (*to* JOHANSSON). Clear out. (JOHANSSON *hesitates.*) Clear out!

JOHANSSON *goes out into the hall. The* OLD MAN *looks round the room; stops amazed in front of the statue.*

OLD MAN. Amelia! It's she! Yes! It's she! (*Wanders round the room, fingering things; arranges his wig in front of the mirror; goes back to the statue.*)

MUMMY (*from the cupboard*). Pretty Poll!

OLD MAN (*starts*). What was that? Is there a parrot in the room? But I don't see one.

MUMMY. Is Jacob there?

OLD MAN. It's a ghost!

MUMMY. Jacob!

OLD MAN. I'm frightened! So this is the kind of thing they've been concealing! (*Looks at a painting, his back towards the cupboard.*) That's him! Him!

MUMMY (*comes up behind the* OLD MAN *and tweaks his wig*). Funny Man! Is it Funny Man?

OLD MAN (*jumps into the air*). God Almighty! Who is it?

MUMMY (*in an ordinary human voice*). Is it Jacob?

OLD MAN. My name *is* Jacob —

MUMMY (*with emotion*). And my name is Amelia.

OLD MAN. No, no, no! Oh, Lord Jesus —

MUMMY. This is how I look now. Yes. And I used to look like that. One lives and learns. I stay in the cupboard mostly, to avoid seeing people — and being seen. What are you looking for in here, Jacob?

OLD MAN. My child. Our child.

MUMMY. She's sitting over there.

OLD MAN. Where?

MUMMY. There. In the hyacinth room.

OLD MAN (*looks at the* DAUGHTER). Yes — it's she! (*Pause.*)

What does her father say? I mean – the Colonel – your
husband –

MUMMY. I lost my temper with him once, and told him everything –

OLD MAN. Yes?

MUMMY. He didn't believe me. He just replied: 'That's what
all wives say when they want to murder their husbands.' It
was a beastly thing to do. His life's a lie too, though. Even
his pedigree. Sometimes I look at the List of Nobility and
think to myself: 'She's got a false birth certificate, like a
little kitchen slut. People get sent to prison for that.'

OLD MAN. Lots of people lie about their birth. You did once –
to me –

MUMMY. My mother made me. I wasn't to blame. But the
crime which you and I committed – you were to blame for
that.

OLD MAN. No it was your husband's fault; he stole my sweet-
heart from me. I was born like that – I can't forgive until
I've punished. To me, that's a command, a duty – I still feel
so.

MUMMY. What are you looking for in this house? What do
you want? How did you get in? Is it my daughter – ? If you
touch her, you shall die.

OLD MAN. I only wish her well.

MUMMY. But you must spare her father. I mean, my husband –

OLD MAN. No!

MUMMY. Then you shall die. In this room, behind that screen –

OLD MAN. That may be. But once I have fastened my teeth
into someone, I cannot let go.

MUMMY. You want her to marry the student. Why? He's
nothing. No money –

OLD MAN. I shall make him rich.

MUMMY. Were you invited for this evening?

OLD MAN. No. But I shall invite myself to this ghost supper.

MUMMY. Do you know who's coming?

OLD MAN. Not for sure.

MUMMY. The baron – the one who lives upstairs – the son-in-
law of the man who was buried this afternoon –

OLD MAN. Oh, the one who's getting divorced so that he can marry the caretaker's daughter! He was once your lover.

MUMMY. And the woman to whom you were once betrothed – and whom my husband seduced –

OLD MAN. A pretty bunch!

MUMMY. Oh, God! If we could die! If we could only die!

OLD MAN. Why do you all keep on meeting?

MUMMY. Our crimes bind us; our secrets, and our guilt. We have tried to break away many times. But we always come back.

OLD MAN. I think I hear the Colonel.

MUMMY. I'll go in to Adèle, then. (*Pause.*) Jacob, mind what you do. Spare him. (*Pause. She goes.*)

The COLONEL *enters, cold and reserved.*

COLONEL. Please be seated.

The OLD MAN *sits, slowly. Pause. The* COLONEL *looks at him.*

You wrote this letter?

OLD MAN. Yes.

COLONEL. Your name is Hummel?

OLD MAN. Yes (*Pause.*)

COLONEL. I know you have purchased all my notes of hand, and that I am therefore in your power. What do you want?

OLD MAN. Payment. In some form.

COLONEL. What form?

OLD MAN. Something quite simple. Let's not talk about money. I merely ask that you tolerate me in your house, as your guest.

COLONEL. If so trifling a service can be of use to you –

OLD MAN. Thank you.

COLONEL. What else?

OLD MAN. Dismiss Bengtsson.

COLONEL. But why should I do that? My trusted servant, who has been with me all his life – who wears his country's medal for loyal and faithful service? Why should I dismiss him?

OLD MAN. He possesses these virtues only in your imagination. He is not the man he appears to be.

COLONEL. Who is?

OLD MAN (*recoils*). True. But Bengtsson must go.

COLONEL. Are you going to decide what happens in my own home?

OLD MAN. Yes. I own everything you see here. Furniture, curtains, china, linen. Other things, too.

COLONEL. What other things?

OLD MAN. Everything. Everything you see. It is all mine.

COLONEL. Very well. All that is yours. But my patent of nobility and my good name – they at least are still mine.

OLD MAN. No. Not even those. (*Pause.*) You're not a nobleman.

COLONEL. How dare you?

OLD MAN (*takes out a paper*). If you read this letter from the College of Heralds you will see that the family whose name you bear has been extinct for a hundred years.

COLONEL (*reads*). I – have heard rumours to this effect, it is true – But I inherited the title from my father – (*Reads.*) No. It is true. You are right. I am not a nobleman. Even that is taken from me. I can no longer wear this ring. Take it. It belongs to you.

OLD MAN (*puts on the ring*). Good. Now let's continue. You're not a Colonel either.

COLONEL. Not a Colonel?

OLD MAN. No. Because of your name you were commissioned colonel in the American Volunteers, but since the Cuban War and the reorganization of the American Army all such commissions have been cancelled.

COLONEL. Is that true?

OLD MAN (*puts his hand towards his pocket*). Would you like to read about it?

COLONEL. No – there's no need. Who are you, that you claim the right to sit there and strip me like this?

OLD MAN. You'll find out. Talking of stripping – I suppose you do know who you really are?

COLONEL. You have the effrontery – !

OLD MAN. Take off your wig and look at yourself in the glass; take out your teeth, shave off your moustaches; get Bengtsson to unlace your corset. Perhaps then a certain footman may recognize himself; who used to sponge food from a certain cook in a certain kitchen –

The COLONEL *reaches towards the bell on the table.*

OLD MAN (*stops him*). Don't touch that bell. Don't call for Bengtsson. If you do, I shall have him arrested. Your guests are arriving. Keep calm, now; we'll go on playing our old parts for a little longer.

COLONEL. Who are you? I seem to recognize the expression in your eyes – and voice –

OLD MAN. Ask no more. Be silent and obey.

STUDENT (*enters and bows to the* COLONEL). Sir!

COLONEL. Welcome, young man. Your noble conduct in this great disaster has made your name a household word, and I count it an honour to be permitted to receive you in my home –

STUDENT. Colonel – my humble origins – your famous name – your noble heritage –

COLONEL. Hm – may I present – Mr. Arkenholz, Mr. Hummel. Will you be so good as to go in and introduce yourself to the ladies? I have a little business to finish with Mr. Hummel.

The STUDENT *is shown into the hyacinth room, where he remains visible, engaged in shy conversation with the* DAUGHTER.

COLONEL. A superb young man – musician – singer – poet – If only he were of noble stock – my peer genealogically – I wouldn't set my face against having him as a – hm, yes –

OLD MAN. As a what?

COLONEL. My daughter –

OLD MAN. *Your* daughter? Talking of her, why does she always sit in there?

COLONEL. She feels a compulsion to sit in the hyacinth room when she isn't out of doors. It's a quirk she has – Ah, here

comes Mademoiselle Beata von Holsteinkrona – a charming
old lady – tremendously wealthy – a great benefactress –
OLD MAN (*to himself*). My true love!

The FIANCÉE *curtsies and sits. The* NOBLEMAN, *a secretive
figure dressed in mourning, enters and sits.*

COLONEL. Baron Skanskorg –

OLD MAN (*aside, without getting up*). I think he's the fellow who
stole those jewels. (*To the* COLONEL.) Let out the mummy,
and the party'll be complete.

COLONEL (*at the doorway to the hyacinth room*). Polly!

MUMMY (*enters*). Funny man!

COLONEL. Shall we have the young people in, too?

OLD MAN. No. Not the young. Let them be spared.

They all sit in a dumb circle.

COLONEL. Shall we take tea?

OLD MAN. Why? None of us likes tea. Why pretend we do?

Pause.

COLONEL. Shall we talk, then?

OLD MAN (*slowly and with pauses*). About the weather, which
we know? Ask after each other's health? We know that, too.
I prefer silence. Then one can hear thoughts, and see the
past. Silence hides nothing. Words conceal. I read the other
day that differences of language arose through the need of
primitive peoples to keep their tribal secrets private. Languages are cyphers; it's only a question of finding the key;
but secrets can be exposed without the key, especially when
it's a question of proving one's parentage. Legal proof is
another matter, of course; a couple of false witnesses can
furnish that – provided their testimonies agree. But in cases
such as the one I have in mind, there are no witnesses, for
nature has endowed man with a sense of shame which seeks
to hide that which should be hid. Nevertheless, the time
sometimes comes when that which is most secret must be
revealed, when the mask is stripped from the deceiver's face,
when the identity of the criminal is exposed. (*Pause. They all*

look at each other in silence.) What a silence! (*Long silence*.)
Here, for example, in this respectable house, this exquisite
home, where beauty, culture and wealth are united – (*Long
silence*.) We who sit here, we know what we are – hm ? – I
don't need to underline that. And you all know me, though
you pretend you don't. In that room sits my daughter – yes,
mine! You know that, too. She has lost the desire to live – she
doesn't know why – this air foul with crime and treachery
and falsehood has withered her. I have tried to find her a
friend through whom she may discover light and warmth –
the light and the warmth that a noble action engenders.
(*Long silence*.) That was why I came to this house; to burn
out the weeds, expose the crimes, balance the ledger, so that
these young people may start life afresh in this home which
I have given them. (*Long silence*.) Now I give you leave to
depart in peace, each of you in your turn. Anyone who stays
I shall have arrested. (*Long silence*.) Listen to the clock
ticking, the clock of death on the wall. Do you hear what
she's saying ? ' 'Tis time – 'tis time'. In a little while, she will
strike, and your time will be up; then you may depart, but
not till then. But before she strikes, she whispers this threat.
Listen! She's warning you! 'The clock – can – strike'. I too,
can strike! (*He strikes the table with his crutch*.) You hear ?

MUMMY (*goes over to the clock and stops the pendulum. Then she
says clearly and earnestly*.) But I can halt time. I can wipe out
the past, undo what has been done. Not with bribes, not
with threats; but through suffering and contrition. (*Goes over
to the* OLD MAN.) We are weak and pitiable creatures; we
know that. We have erred, and sinned, like all mortals. We
are not what we seem, for our true selves live within us,
condemning our failings. But that you, Jacob Hummel, sit
here wearing your false name and judge us, proves you worse
than us, wretched as we are. You are not what you seem
any more than we are. You are a robber of souls, for you
robbed me of mine with your false promises; you murdered
the consul they buried today, you strangled him with your
notes of hand; and now you have stolen the student's soul for
a feigned debt of his father, who never owed you a penny.

The OLD MAN *has tried to rise and interrupt her, but has fallen back in his chair, and shrunk small. During what follows, he shrinks smaller and smaller.*

MUMMY. But there is a black spot in your life. I don't know the full truth about it; but I can guess. And I fancy Bengtsson knows. (*Rings the bell on the table.*)

OLD MAN. No! Not Bengtsson! Not him!

MUMMY. Ah! Then he does know. (*Rings again.*)

The little MILKMAID *appears in the door leading from the hall, unseen by anyone except the* OLD MAN, *who cringes in terror. The* MILKMAID *disappears as* BENGTSSON *enters.*

MUMMY. Bengtsson, do you know this man?

BENGTSSON. Yes; I know him, and he knows me. Life has its ups and downs; he has served in my house, as I now serve in this one. He hung around my cook for two years. So that he could get away by three o'clock, we had to have dinner ready by two; and then we had to make do with the warmed-up remains of what he'd left. He drank the juice from the meat, too, so that we had to eke out what was left with water. He sat there like a vampire sucking all the goodness out of our home, and left us skeletons; then, when we called the cook a thief, he had us put in prison. Later, I met this man in Hamburg, under another name. He'd become a usurer — another kind of bloodsucker; besides which, he was accused of having lured a young girl out on the ice to drown her, because she'd been witness to a crime he was afraid might get discovered —

MUMMY (*puts her hand over the* OLD MAN's *face.*) You see yourself. Now give me your notes of hand. And the deeds of the house.

JOHANSSON *appears in the door leading to the hall, and watches the scene with interest, realizing it means his release from slavery. The* OLD MAN *takes out a bundle of papers and throws them on the table.*

MUMMY (*strokes the* OLD MAN's *back*). Pretty parrot. Jacob? Jacob?

OLD MAN (*in a parrot's voice*). Jacob's here! Cacadora! Dora!
MUMMY. Can the clock strike?
OLD MAN (*clucks*). The clock can strike. (*Imitates a cuckoo clock.*) Cuc-koo, cuc-koo, cuc-koo.
MUMMY (*opens the cupboard door*). Now the clock has struck. Get up and go into the cupboard where I have sat for twenty years, mourning our folly. In it there hangs a rope. Let it remind you of the rope with which you strangled the Consul upstairs, and thought to strangle your benefactor. Go!

The OLD MAN *goes into the cupboard. The* MUMMY *shuts the door.*

Bengtsson! Put out the screen. The death screen.

BENGTSSON *puts the screen in front of the door.*

It is accomplished. May God have mercy on his soul.
ALL. Amen.

Long silence.

In the hyacinth room, the DAUGHTER *becomes visible. She plays on a harp as the student sings.*

SONG (*preceded by a prelude*).
I saw the sun.
I seemed to see the Hidden One.
Man reaps as he sows.
The doer of good shall receive blessing.
Answer not with evil what was done in anger.
Repay with goodness him thou hast robbed.
He who hath done no wrong hath nought to fear.
Innocence is goodness.

A room somewhat bizarrely decorated in Oriental style. Hyacinths of all colours, everywhere. On the top of the tiled stove sits a large statue of Buddha, with a flat root on his knees. Out of it rises the stalk of an Ascalon flower, with its globe of white, star-shaped petals.

Upstage right a door leads out to the round drawing room, where the COLONEL *and the* MUMMY *sit silent, doing nothing. Part of the death screen is also visible. On the left, a door leads out to the kitchen and pantry.*

The STUDENT *and the* DAUGHTER *are at the table, she seated at her harp, he standing.*

DAUGHTER. Sing for my flowers.

STUDENT. Is the hyacinth your flower?

DAUGHTER. It is my only flower. You love the hyacinth, too?

STUDENT. Above all other flowers. I love its slim figure, which rises erect and virginal from its roots, rests on water, and sinks its pure, white tendrils in the colourless stream. I love its colours; the white of snow and innocence, the honey-gold of sweetness, the rose-pink of youth, the scarlet of maturity; but above all the blue – the blue of deep eyes, of dew, of steadfastness. I love them all, more than gold or pearls. I have loved hyacinths ever since I was a child. I have worshipped them, because they embody everything I lack. And yet –

DAUGHTER. Yes.

STUDENT. My love is unrequited, for these beautiful flowers hate me.

DAUGHTER. Why do you say that?

STUDENT. Their perfume, strong and clean with the first zephyrs of spring, which have passed over melting snow, confuses my senses, deafens me, blinds me, drives me from my room, shoots me with poisoned arrows which sadden my heart and set my head aflame. Don't you know the legend of this flower?

DAUGHTER. Tell me.

[STUDENT. First, I will tell you its meaning. The root, resting on the water or buried in the soil, is the earth. The stalk shoots up, straight as the axis of the world, and on the top of it rest the star-flowers with their six-headed petals.

DAUGHTER. Stars over the earth! How beautiful! Where did you find that vision, how did you see it?]

STUDENT. [Where? In your eyes.] It is an image of the world.

183

Buddha sits with the earth on his knees, brooding over it, watching it grow outwards and upwards, transforming itself into a heaven. This unhappy earth shall become a heaven! It is that that Buddha awaits.

[DAUGHTER. Yes – now I see it! Is not the snow-flower starred with six points like the hyacinth lily?

STUDENT. Yes. Snow-flowers are falling stars –

DAUGHTER. And the snowdrop is a snow-star, risen from the snow.

STUDENT. But Sirius, the largest and most beautiful of the stars of the firmament in its gold and red, is the narcissus with its gold and red cup and its six white petals –

DAUGHTER. Have you seen the Ascalon flower?

STUDENT. Yes – yes, I have. It carries its blooms in a sphere like the sphere of heaven, strewn with white flowers.]

DAUGHTER. [Yes! Ah, God – how wonderful!] Who first imagined this vision?

STUDENT. You.

DAUGHTER. You.

STUDENT. You and I together. We have given birth to a vision. We are wed.

DAUGHTER. Not yet.

STUDENT. What remains?

DAUGHTER. The waiting, the trials, the patience.

STUDENT. Good! Try me. (*Pause.*) Tell me – why do your parents sit so silently in there, never saying a word?

DAUGHTER. They have nothing to say to each other, for neither will believe what the other says. My father once said: 'What is the point of our talking? We cannot deceive each other.'

STUDENT. How horrible.

DAUGHTER. Here comes the cook. Look at her! How big and fat she is!

STUDENT. What does she want?

DAUGHTER. She wants to ask me about dinner. I look after the house while my mother is ill –

STUDENT. Must we bother about what happens in the kitchen?

DAUGHTER. We have to eat. Look at the cook – I can't look at her –

STUDENT. Who is this ogress?

DAUGHTER. One of the Hummels – that breed of vampires. She is devouring us –

STUDENT. Why don't you dismiss her?

DAUGHTER. She won't go. We have no control over her. She is our punishment for our sins. Can't you see? We are wasting away. We are being consumed.

STUDENT. Doesn't she give you any food?

DAUGHTER. Oh, yes. She cooks us many dishes, but there is no nourishment in them. She boils the meat till it is nothing but sinews and water, while she herself drinks the juice from it. When she roasts she cooks the meat till the goodness is gone; she drinks the gravy and the blood. Everything she touches loses its moisture, as though her eyes sucked it dry. She drinks the coffee and leaves us the dregs, she drinks the wine from the bottles and fills them with water –

STUDENT. Drive her out of the house!

DAUGHTER. We can't.

STUDENT. Why not?

DAUGHTER. We don't know. She won't go. No one has any control over her. She has drained the strength from us.

STUDENT. Can I send her away?

DAUGHTER. No. It is ordained. She must stay with us. She asks what we will have for dinner. I reply. She objects. And in the end, she does as she pleases.

STUDENT. Let her decide the meals, then.

DAUGHTER. She will not.

STUDENT. This is a strange house. It is bewitched.

DAUGHTER. Yes. Ah! She turned away when she saw you!

COOK (*in the doorway*). No, that wasn't why. (*Grins, showing her teeth.*)

STUDENT. Get out!

COOK. When I feel like it. (*Pause.*) Now I feel like it. (*Goes.*)

DAUGHTER. Never mind. You must learn patience. She is one of the trials we have to endure in this house. We have a maid, too. We have to dust everywhere after her.

STUDENT. My head reels. *Cor in aethere*. Sing to me!

DAUGHTER. Wait!

185

STUDENT. Sing to me!

DAUGHTER. Be patient. This room is called the room of trial. It is beautiful to look at, but consists only of imperfections –

STUDENT. Incredible. But we must turn a blind eye to them. It is beautiful, but a little cold. Why don't you have a fire lit?

DAUGHTER. Because it smokes.

STUDENT. Can't you have the chimney cleaned?

DAUGHTER. That doesn't help. You see that desk?

STUDENT. It's very beautiful.

DAUGHTER. But it won't stand straight. Each day I put a cork disc under its leg, but the maid takes it away when she dusts, and I have to cut a new one. Every morning the pen is clogged with ink, and the inkwell too. I have to wash them after she's gone, every day of my life. (*Pause.*) What's the worst thing you know?

STUDENT. Counting laundry. Ugh!

DAUGHTER. That's what I have to do. Ugh!

STUDENT. What else?

DAUGHTER. To be woken in the middle of the night, and have to get up to fasten the window-catch, because the maid's forgotten to.

STUDENT. What else?

DAUGHTER. To climb up a ladder and mend the cord of the damper on the stove, when she's wrenched it loose.

STUDENT. What else?

DAUGHTER. To clean up after her, and dust behind her, and light the fire after her – she only puts in the wood. To open the damper, dry the glasses, re-lay the table, uncork the bottles, open the windows to air the rooms, re-make my bed, clean the water carafe when it grows green with slime, buy matches and soap, which we're always out of, dry the lamps and trim the wicks so that they won't smoke – I have to fill them myself so that they won't go out when we have guests –

STUDENT. Sing to me!

DAUGHTER. Wait! First the toil, the toil of holding the dirt of life at bay.

STUDENT. But you're rich. Why don't you keep two maids?

DAUGHTER. It wouldn't help, even if we had three. Life is hard
– sometimes I grow tired. Imagine if there were a nursery
as well!

STUDENT. The greatest joy of all –

DAUGHTER. The most expensive. Is life worth so much
trouble?

STUDENT. It depends what one wants in return. I would
shrink from nothing to win your hand.

DAUGHTER. Don't talk like that. You can never win me.

STUDENT. Why not?

DAUGHTER. You mustn't ask.

Pause.

STUDENT. You dropped your bracelet out of the window.

DAUGHTER. Because my hand has grown so thin –

Pause. The COOK *appears, with a Japanese bottle in her hand.*

DAUGHTER. It's she who is devouring me. Devouring us all.

STUDENT. What's she got in her hand?

DAUGHTER. The colorite bottle with the scorpion lettering. It
contains soya, to make water into stock. We use it instead of
gravy, and to cook cabbage in, and to make turtle soup –

STUDENT. Get out!

COOK. You drain the goodness out of us, and we drain it from
you. We take the blood and give you back the water – with
the colorite. This is colorite. I'm going now, but I'm staying
in this house as long as I want. (*Goes.*)

STUDENT. Why does Bengtsson wear a medal?

DAUGHTER. For faithful service.

STUDENT. Has he no faults?

DAUGHTER. Yes, very great ones. But you don't get medals
for them.

They both laugh.

STUDENT. You have many secrets in this house.

DAUGHTER. Like everyone else. Let us keep ours.

Pause.

STUDENT. Do you love honesty?

DAUGHTER. Yes. Quite.

STUDENT. Sometimes I'm seized with a passionate desire to say everything I think; but I know that if people were really honest the world would come to an end. (*Pause.*) The other day I was at a funeral. In the church. It was very impressive, very beautiful.

DAUGHTER. Was it Hummel's?

STUDENT. Yes. My benefactor. At the head of the coffin stood an old friend of the dead man, holding the funeral mace. The priest impressed me deeply by his dignified bearing and his moving sermon. I wept. We all wept. Afterwards we went to a hotel. There I learned that the man with the mace had been in love with the dead man's son. (*The* DAUGHTER *looks at him, not understanding.*) And that the dead man had borrowed money from his son's admirer. (*Pause.*) And the next day the priest was arrested for stealing from the church funds. Pretty, isn't it?

DAUGHTER. Horrible.

Pause.

STUDENT. Do you know what I'm thinking? About you?

DAUGHTER. Don't tell me. If you do, I shall die.

STUDENT. I must, or I shall die.

DAUGHTER. In madhouses, people say everything they think.

STUDENT. I know. My father died in a madhouse.

DAUGHTER. Was he sick?

STUDENT. No. He was perfectly well; just mad. He only showed it once; I'll tell you how. He was surrounded, as we all are, by a circle of – associates; he called them friends, the word was shorter and more convenient. They were a gang of scoundrels, of course; most people are. But he had to have someone to talk to, he couldn't bear to be alone. One doesn't ordinarily tell people what one thinks of them, and neither did he. He knew they were false and treacherous; but he was a wise man, and had been well brought up, so he was always polite to everyone. But one day he gave a great party. It was in the evening; he was tired after his day's work, and tired with the strain of listening to his guests and exchanging spiteful gossip with them.

The DAUGHTER *shudders.*

Well, he rapped on the table for silence, and stood up with his glass to make a speech. Then the safety-catch flew off, and as he talked he stripped the company naked, flinging their hypocrisy in their faces. Then he sat down exhausted on the middle of the table, and told them all to go to hell.

DAUGHTER. Oh!

STUDENT. I was there, and I shall never forget what happened next. My mother hit him, he hit her, the guests rushed for the door – and Father was taken to the madhouse, where he died. (*Pause.*) Water which has remained stationary and silent for too long becomes rotten. It's the same with this house. Something has rotted here, too. And when I saw you walk through the door for the first time, I thought it was Paradise. I stood there one Sunday morning, and gazed in through the windows. I saw a Colonel who was not a Colonel, I found a noble benefactor who turned out to be a crook, and had to hang himself, I saw a mummy that was not a mummy, and a maid. . . . Where is virginity to be found? Or beauty? Only in flowers and trees . . . and in my head when I am dressed in my Sunday clothes. Where are faith and honour to be found? In fairy tales and games that children play. Where can I find anything that will fulfil its promise? Only in my imagination. Your flowers have poisoned me, and I have poisoned you in return. I asked you to be my wife and share my home, we wrote poems, we sang and played. And then the cook came in. *Sursum corda!* Try once more to strike fire and purple from your golden harp! Try, I beg you! I command you – on my knees. Then I shall do it myself. (*Takes the harp, but no sound comes from the strings.*) It is deaf and dumb. Why should the most beautiful flowers be the most poisonous? It is a curse that hangs over all creation, all life. Why would you not be my bride? Because the source of life is poisoned in you. Now I can feel that vampire in the kitchen beginning to suck my blood – perhaps she's a Lamia who lives on the blood of children – it's always in the kitchen that children's hearts are nipped, if it hasn't already happened in the bedroom. There are poisons which blind and poisons which open the eyes. I must have been born with the second kind in my veins, because I can't see beauty in ugliness or call evil good – I can't! Jesus Christ descended into hell when he wandered through this madhouse, this brothel, this morgue which we call earth. The madmen killed him when he tried to set them free, and released a robber instead; the robber always gets the sympathy. Alas for us all, alas! O Saviour of the World, save us! We are dying.

The DAUGHTER *has crumpled in her chair. She rings.* BENGTS-SON *enters.*

DAUGHTER. Bring the screen. Quickly! I am dying.

BENGTSSON *comes back with the screen, which he opens and places in front of the* DAUGHTER.

STUDENT. The deliverer cometh. Welcome, Thou pale and gentle One. And you, beautiful, unhappy, innocent creature, who must suffer for the guilt of others, sleep! Sleep dreamlessly, and when you wake again may you be greeted by a sun that will not burn, in a home without dust, by friends ignorant of dishonour, by a love that knows no imperfections. O wise and gentle Buddha, who sitteth waiting for a heaven to rise up out of the earth, grant us patience in our time of trial, and grant us purity of will, that thy hopes may be fulfilled.

The harp's strings begin to whisper. The room becomes filled with a white light.

SONG.
I saw the sun.
I seemed to see the Hidden One.
Man reaps as he sows.
The doer of good shall receive blessing.
Answer not with evil what was done in anger.
Repay with goodness him thou hast robbed.

He who hath done no wrong hath nought to fear.
Innocence is goodness.

A moaning is heard from behind the screen.

STUDENT. Unhappy child, born into this world of delusion,
guilt, suffering and death, this world that is for ever changing,
for ever erring, for ever in pain! The Lord of Heaven be
merciful to you on your journey.

The room disappears. Böcklin's painting of the Island of the
Dead *appears in the background. Soft music, calm and gently
melancholy, is heard from the island.*

The bold brackets on pp 183-4 indicate suggested cuts for performance.

Methuen Drama also publish a second volume of Strindberg's plays (a third will be published in May 1991) and six volumes of Ibsen's plays, all translated and introduced by Michael Meyer, and in the same series:

STRINDBERG

PLAYS: TWO
A Dream Play, The Dance of Death, The Stronger

PLAYS: THREE
Master Olof, Creditors, To Damascus (Part I)
(Publication May 1991)

IBSEN

PLAYS: ONE
Ghosts, The Wild Duck, The Master Builder

PLAYS: TWO
A Doll's House, An Enemy of the People, Hedda Gabler

PLAYS: THREE
Rosmersholm, Little Eyolf, The Lady from the Sea

PLAYS: FOUR
John Gabriel Borkman, The Pillars of Society, When We Dead Awaken

PLAYS: FIVE
Brand, Emperor and Galilean

PLAYS: SIX
Peer Gynt, The Pretenders